LITERATURE AND THERAPY

LITERATURE AND THERAPY
A Systemic View

Liz Burns

KARNAC

First published in 2009 by
Karnac Books Ltd
118 Finchley Road
London NW3 5HT

British Library Cataloguing in Publication Data

A C.I.P. for this book is available from the British Library

ISBN-13: 978-1-85575-594-9

Typeset by Vikatan Publishing Solutions (p) Ltd., Chennai, India

Printed in Great Britain

www.karnacbooks.com

This book is dedicated to all the readers and writers whose contributions grace its chapters, and to my parents, John and Marjorie, who would have loved to live long enough to see it.

There are bridges between one sort of thought and the other ... the artists and poets are specifically concerned with these bridges. It is not that art is the expression of the unconscious, but rather that it is concerned with the relation between the levels of mental process.

(Bateson, 1972, p. 464)

The function of literature as art is to open us to dilemmas, to the hypothetical, to the range of possible worlds that a text can refer to ... It is our only hope against the long gray night.

(Bruner, 1986, p. 159)

CONTENTS

ACKNOWLEDGEMENTS

My grateful thanks go to everyone who has contributed to the development of the ideas advanced in the following pages. This includes the participants in the study which launched the enterprise, and all who have subsequently taken part in groups and day-to-day conversations with me on the subject of literary reading. The clients, colleagues and trainees whose dilemmas and insights are represented in the vignettes have given me more help and inspiration than I had any right to expect. I hope they will enjoy reading what I have made of what they gave.

I owe a special debt of gratitude to all the professional colleagues who have been generous with their thoughts, feelings and responses to the ideas developed here. In particular, Rudi Dallos, Gina Wisker and Gillie Bolton have been wise and encouraging mentors and friends from the outset.

A family therapist like me really appreciates the importance of a lively and supportive family. Mine has done very well by me, and thanks are due to Patrick, Daniel, Joseph and Hannah, who have supplied interested and informed comment and have kept my spirits up with love and humour.

Finally, I would like to acknowledge the help of my husband, Mike. His excellent reading skills, generously given, have made all the difference. Without his unfailing practical and emotional support, this project would have been unlikely to see the light of day.

ABOUT THE AUTHOR

Liz Burns is a family therapist of many years' experience. Currently she works as a Consultant Family Therapist in the Child and Adolescent Mental Health Service in Oxfordshire and Buckinghamshire Mental Health Trust. She is also Convenor of the Intermediate Course in Family Therapy and Systemic Practice in Plymouth, a partnership between Plymouth Primary Care Trust and the University of Plymouth.

Her PhD research, completed in 2003 and entitled "An exploration of the place of literary reading in family therapists' personal and professional development", is the starting point of the current volume. She has contributed reviews and articles on literary topics to *Context*, the news magazine of the Association for Family Therapy, since the early 1990s. A paper entitled "The Rainbow Bridge: an approach to family systems via *Howards End*" was printed in the *Journal of Family Therapy* in 1995 and a further paper, co-written with Rudi Dallos and entitled "A different world? Literary reading in family therapists' personal and professional development" has been submitted this year.

A journey of discovery

"Literature is news that STAYS NEWS"

(Ezra Pound, *ABC of Reading*, 1934)

More than a decade of thinking has gone into *Literature and Therapy: a Systemic View*. In the early 90s, having qualified as a family therapist, I began to develop ideas about the relationship of literature with the theory and practices of my new discipline. This book is a tribute to the many people who have helped me. I've followed a hunch and found it paid off, and I want to share my conclusions and my questions with as wide a range of people as possible. So this is a book for them, but it is also a book for me, bearing in mind the wise saying that I don't know what I think until I've written it. Being any kind of psychotherapist is a demanding task and I would like colleagues to share in the exhilaration of finding that a tempting but divergent path actually leads somewhere. There are fascinating destinations in view, but the journey is its own reward. *Literature and Therapy: a Systemic View* takes the journey as its predominant metaphor.

One of my initial inspirations was to discover that "talking literature" was a safe and productive way of sharing ideas on an equal footing with colleagues from different disciplines and theoretical orientations. It is a short step to bridge the gap between professionals and lay people by "talking literature", in both therapeutic and more general contexts. A guided, focused discussion of, say, *Jane Eyre* could bring together "looked after" young people, adoptive and foster parents, social workers looking for predominantly practical solutions, and psychotherapists of all kinds concerned for the emotional wellbeing of children, families, carers and professionals. The possibilities are exciting. All that is required is some flexibility and skill on the part of the facilitator, together with a confidence that working in, and with, the metaphors of literature can produce worthwhile results. Better still, working with literary examples enables a quality of sharing, using both head and heart, which is not readily achieved by other methods.

Of course, participants also need to be willing to read, but the extracts can be brief and supported by visual material, as in graphic novels, comics or video tapes. Stories may be told in many different ways, using a variety of literary forms, and almost anyone will admit to having a favourite "resonant" song. Literature opens up possibilities in the strangest places, e.g. secure hospitals (Cox, 1992; Cox & Theilgaard, 1994), prisons, the juvenile justice system and marginalised groups (see www.escapeartists.co.uk; also "Poetry Places" at www.poetrysociety. org.uk/content/archives/places). It also works in the most unexpected ways. Who could predict, for example, the unique web of connections which one group made between T.S. Eliot's overcoat, the way in which a trainee felt she had "talked down" to the mother of a family in her supervision group, the death of a friend, and the comforting words of the medieval mystic Julian of Norwich: "all shall be well and all shall be well and all manner of thing shall be well"?

Broadening the theory base of systemic psychotherapy

Received wisdom in systemic psychotherapy circles holds that the systemic paradigm (or epistemology, as Bateson liked to call it) grew out of a reaction against the predominance of psychodynamic theory in the understanding and addressing of personal growth, health and psychological healing. This belief has done well by a generation of family therapists, but there is a need now to explore common ground, not only with other therapeutic approaches but with other traditional means of sharing experience socially. Literature is in the forefront of such methods. That is what literature is for.

Currently, we cannot decide whether our social fabric is full of rich diversity or fundamentally fractured. In any case we reject the tyranny of binary exclusivity, that is, "either-or" thinking. Yet psychotherapists must try to engage in meaning-making dialogue with anyone who fetches up at their door, especially those defined as clients. Since literature is a basic cultural resource, learning how to operate inside it and link with others through it may be an overdue priority. I have always thought of family therapy as interdisciplinary in its concepts and practices. I work in the British National Health Service, where family therapy is currently defined (broadly) as a "psychological therapy". Early developers lived alongside, and drew on, anthropology for inspiration. For example, I remember considering in some depth what the ceremonies of the Iatmul people of New Guinea (Bateson, 1972) had to say to us about the conduct of families and groups in late 20th century Britain. Biologists and philosophers have been recruited in because of their wise sayings or their ability to make us question what we think. Narrative enjoys considerable popularity as a metaphor which suggests useful and engaging therapeutic methods, but other literary phenomena and practices have been relatively neglected. Redressing this balance may mean that we begin to draw more systematically upon literary texts and theory, and notice that we have more than a little in common with those working in disciplines like cultural studies.

Encouraging the reader in the therapist and the therapist in the reader

Literary reading, or that activity which links different levels of mental process through the medium of poetry, novels and drama, bears a striking resemblance to psychotherapy process. In both, the making and transformation of meaning through dialogue is basic, and the medium is language. Both require engagement which is multi-layered, combining intellect and emotions and openness to implicit as well as explicit communication. Both imply reciprocal engagement between conversational partners, or between participants and text. Whilst there are obvious differences between reading and face-to-face conversation, it may be argued that therapeutic conversation, with its deliberate use of indeterminacies (e.g. open questions) and conscious questioning of set agendas and expected outcomes, may actually be closer to literary reading than to many other forms of social intercourse.

It was my perception of the analogy between reading and therapeutic process which first alerted me to the mutual enrichment which can result from the linking of the two. If I could learn more about my relationship with the world from reading, then why should the techniques of reading not be applied in some way to my therapy practice? If I could push the limits of understanding through critical engagement with literature then why not try to apply these "literary" practices to my work and "texts" of therapeutic interchanges? Why not go further still and ask literary texts themselves to help "interrogate" topics of therapeutic importance?

Exploring the territory

As my initial interest grew stronger, I explored these ideas in a variety of ways: survey and interviews with systemic psychotherapists; group exercises and their analysis; reading and writing exercises of my own. My enquiry soon became part of a fast expanding web of literature-aided consciousness. It emerged that people could discover profound and influential traces of reading experiences from the past, and could also recognise the significance of these in their current dealings with others. New literary encounters could be applied to growing personal and professional development, individually and in groups. Literary metaphors, and the metaphor of literature, could be used to aid informal thinking and the building of theory, as well as to strengthen emotional flexibility and responsiveness. In systemic psychotherapy contexts, the value of reader as therapist and therapist as reader became progressively clarified. This was especially so in personal/professional development (PPD) aspects of training and in continuing professional development (CPD) for qualified therapists.

I met a lot of people, some naïve and other experienced in therapy, who loved literature. There were some who couldn't get enough of stories, and others who didn't care particularly about character or plot but relished literary uses of language. There were others again who most valued the "feel" of an imaginative or reflective space, marking this for themselves in the look, smell and touch of books. Some cared chiefly about the sound of poetry and its emotional impact, and others liked the intellectual struggle in trying to pin down the meaning. Some people felt literature spoke most eloquently to them through the songs they played whilst driving in their cars. Most were surprised at the level of personal significance attaching to landmark texts from their past, whether serious or seemingly trivial.

Literature: love it or hate it

I began to live with, and in, literature when I was at school. This does not mean I read particularly fast, well, or discerningly. In fact, I have always been a slow reader whose attention is easily distracted. I have a taste for sensation and the macabre, and this has led me down paths which are predominantly trodden by gloomy teenagers and slightly eccentric academics. I love detective stories, less for the puzzles than for the atmosphere. A good one is, to me, like a comfy armchair just made for reading. With the right book, I could be lost for hours, living in a story or wandering through the imaginative landscape of a poem. I had good teachers on the whole, and like-minded friends who would eagerly discuss what we had read and how we felt about it. We were trained to use our critical faculties, and taught a technical vocabulary in which to express and develop our thoughts. This went alongside quite careful teaching of grammar and syntax. We parsed sentences and knew our adjectives from our adverbs. I do not think we were asked, even in the 1960s, to seek out the "real" meaning of anything, but to reflect on the relative merits of different "readings". All of this gave a basis for literary study which was "firm but fair", neither too regimented nor as reductive as that experienced by some of my contemporaries. On the other hand, it was also neither burdened nor enriched by the developments in theory which came later.

Not everyone has had similar advantages. Not everyone is in a position to relate to written literature. We are beginning to understand and appreciate not only the advantages to be gained from literacy but also the degree of social disenfranchisement suffered by those who cannot read and write, through, for example, the work of the National Literacy Trust (www.literacytrust.org.uk). The therapists who participated in my explorations were adamant in their unwillingness to impose their ideas or values on clients. Some saw the deliberate use of literature in therapy as a form of imposition, whilst others took the opposite view: that what had added value to their lives and careers might also do the same for clients, and it was inappropriate to withhold such resources. I propose that using literature (and we are talking about the literature of any and every relevant culture here) actually enables powerful therapists to take a step outside their customary hierarchical position and allow themselves to be inducted into the world of whatever "other" they are meeting. Using literature to mediate dialogue and meaning-making tends to the externalisation of issues or dilemmas and is, therefore, a powerful ally of collaborative therapy and the de-centred therapist.

Some people, however, just do not think literature is for them. This may be because of aversive experiences in earlier life, usually in education. It may also be because literature is defined too narrowly—perhaps through over-emphasis on the "literary canon" and the belief that "popular" reading is an inferior activity with little to offer. In fact, the 21st century offers a rich array of popular cultural products in the arts, and the boundaries between, say, novels and films are increasingly permeable.

It is also clear that some people reject literature which sets out to create stories of, or interact with, imaginary worlds. This may be simply because they find information about, say, machines more imaginatively stimulating and emotionally satisfying than narratives about people. This may also be true of abstract topics. It is an interesting question how far an insistence on story books accounts for the falling off in boys' interest in reading in middle childhood. On the other hand, it is easy to see that too much difference between the content of literature and people's lives is inimical to the development of a taste for reading fiction. Harper Lee writes of the children of rural Alabama and their teacher, who assumes that a story about talking cats will help her engage with her new class of five-year-olds:

> Miss Caroline began the day by reading us a story about cats. The cats had long conversations with one another; they wore cunning little clothes and lived in a warm house beneath a

kitchen stove. By the time Mrs Cat called the drug store for an order of chocolate malted mice the class was wriggling like a bucketful of Catawba worms. Miss Caroline seemed unaware that the ragged, denim-shirted and floursack-skirted first grade, most of whom chopped cotton and fed hogs from the time they were able to walk, were immune to imaginative literature. (Harper Lee 'To Kill a Mockingbird' 1960/1997, p. 18)

Reflexivity

I owe a debt of gratitude to all the writers referred to in this book. They have helped me to think about myself and to put my personal and professional experience in a wider context. They have done more than this, however. They, or more precisely, their writings and my relationship with them, have pulled and pushed me, setting me off in unforeseen directions, transforming my thoughts and feelings as I worked alongside them. Current psychotherapy practice places high value on conscious self consciousness, or reflexivity. In qualitative enquiry, credibility is only established if the contribution of the "observer" is accounted for.

One way of enlisting literary texts to reflect and develop a reflexive stance is to trace the influence of particular texts at different life stages. This amounts to an individual's "reading history", which can highlight enduring attachments and key sources of personal meaning. Another way is to select a text which seems to resonate with a dilemma or stage of learning and follow the ways in which a close critical reading of the text can help to illuminate the issue in question. This may sound fanciful or unduly complex, but is actually very easy and exciting when working within the metaphorical mode which literature characteristically offers. The kind of fusion which takes place between the life situation and the literary one releases creative energy, whilst the form of the text gives structure and meaning to the process. I found, for example, that a reading of Tennyson's "Lady of Shalott" gave stimulus and shape to my thinking about the roots of my relationship with literary study. Virginia Woolf's To the Lighthouse exemplified the struggle to convey interior experience into the minds of others, in language. It left me with an enduring fancy for lighthouses, and an abiding desire to explore subjectivity and intersubjectivity through reading and writing.

I hope this book will prompt its readers to experiment and explore themselves and their therapeutic practice in the company of writers and commentators who come at the vicissitudes of human life from a different direction. The work of a helping professional can be absorbing and rewarding. Too often, however, it can be personally draining and performed in difficult circumstances. Burnout is always a risk, especially if the helper is cut off from sources of personal and professional support. In most human cultures literature is there, waiting to offer inspiration.

A note about the use of the title "therapist" and the "systemic view"

Some people may find my use of the term "therapist" rather vague and over-inclusive. This may reflect the times in which we live, an in-between time in the UK, when at least two related but contradictory processes are in operation in relation to the accessing and provision of "therapeutic" services. There is on the one hand unprecedented access to information on the internet and political commitment to "choice" in healthcare. Consumers are increasingly accustomed to defining (rightly or wrongly) the sort of help they need. On the other hand, practitioners who consider themselves experts in their field by reason of training skills, and knowledge, seek to limit the use of their professional titles through regulation and professional registration. Further complexity is added when "non-expert" stances are favoured by therapists, and therapeutic models construe clients as "experts" in their own lives. I have chosen to step aside from these big questions and use the term "therapist" to refer to any helping professional who is engaged in broadly health-promoting activities. I mostly have in mind psychological therapies in mental health settings, but I would not want to exclude practitioners whose focus may be less on language and more on embodied experience: medical practitioners, for example, who also feel that how their patients think, feel and live their lives is important.

I also want to be inclusive about levels of training and experience. In the NHS mental health services I know, there is currently a move towards increasing the deployment of more generic practitioners and limiting the number of more specialised, highly trained people who are, amongst other things, more expensive to employ. A longer story attaches to this than we can attend to here. Suffice to say, this book is for people at all levels of experience and as much for the generic as for the more specialised worker.

I have selected a "systemic view" because I am trained, and have practised for so many years, as a family therapist that I doubt my ability to take any other view convincingly. I also think of it as a view which lends itself to inclusiveness and is capable of being expressed in language which is relatively jargon-free.

A note about literary texts

Literary texts are an essential feature of forthcoming chapters and exercises. As therapists we are accustomed to taking great care to treat the words of our clients and colleagues with respect. This is also important with literary texts. Some, of course, are entwined with our own consciousness—so much so that a visitor to a performance of *Macbeth* was heard to express disappointment that Shakespeare made use of so many common phrases and sayings, even clichés, in his writings. Others are much more unfamiliar, maybe even somewhat inaccessible. All those I am using are in the public arena through publication, but they are also art works and deserving of sincere engagement—both challenging and appreciative.

I am not supplying large amounts of literary text in this book but rather pointing you, the reader, in the appropriate direction (see Appendix 3). There are at least two reasons for this, the first being that writers are understandably reluctant to relinquish control of their work and how it is reproduced and passed on. The work is their intellectual property. Copyright laws support them in this, and it is simply impractical in a book like this to provide large amounts of other people's writing. The second reason is that the texts referred to in this book are available on the library shelves, in booksellers, charity shops and online. They are often in collections and anthologies where other poems, other passages of the story, and so on, are also there to be browsed. Early on, when I had just begun to talk about literature with clients and colleagues, I drew the attention of a woman with whom I had been working to the poems of Adrienne Rich. I lent her my copy of collected works with the idea that she would read a particular poem (of my choice) and find something provocative and useful in it. The next time we met, she said that she had quite liked the poem I suggested, but in fact it was the poem on the opposite page which had cried out for her attention. It spoke strongly to her of the personal experience of abuse, resilience and recovery. Browsing had brought her into contact with a poem which came to mean a great deal to her and to me.

A note about vignettes

The reader will find numerous vignettes and clinical examples. These are all based on accumulated clinical and professional experience and are composites which I have created to illustrate the points I am trying to make. My vignettes are specially constructed for the purpose and fictionalised. I think this is important for a couple of reasons. I have long felt that although we need to know how our ideas measure up to actual experience, the use of case examples is in itself an intervention into the lives of others. As such it needs appropriate informed consent. I wanted to use lots of examples, and yet did not feel equal to the task of finding all the people I might have mentioned in order to ask permission, remembering and sticking carefully to the facts, being scrupulous not to give a different slant to something with hindsight, and so on. More importantly, however, I decided to use examples which are essentially fictitious and which carry concentrations of "truth" which are not otherwise available. This technique accords fully with the aim of highlighting the truth of fiction. I hope that readers will recognise thoughts, feelings and dilemmas which are true to life without feeling that personal space has been invaded.

Exercises

Each of the forthcoming chapters will conclude with a recommended exercise, the details of which are given in Appendix 4. These exercises suggest a practical framework within which readers can practise the use of new ideas. Exercises will not immediately give you answers to pressing questions. Whilst they may promote the development of techniques, they are more oriented to the development of generic abilities, not to the solution of specific problems. In our work we routinely warn ourselves and others to mistrust the illusion of "easy answers". The complex personal and interpersonal conundrums of therapeutic work are not susceptible to simple remedies. The exercises encourage readers to wander in the imaginative landscape of literature just to see what is there, no matter that these activities may seem alien and impractical in our days of evidence and "the bottom line". There is the danger that if we neglect our ability to "stand and stare" (*Leisure*, by W.H. Davies), we lose something essential to our humanity. Davies suggests that "a poor life" is the result. A basic condition of all the exercises in this book is that we deliberately assume an open posture of curiosity and have a go!

PART I

STARTING OUT

CHAPTER ONE

Starting out with literature

"Where shall I begin, please your Majesty?" he asked.
"Begin at the beginning," the King said, gravely, "and go on until you come to the end: then stop."
(Lewis Carroll, *Alice's Adventures in Wonderland*, 1865)

"That reminds me of a story."
(Gregory Bateson, *Mind and Nature: A Necessary Unity*, 1988)

A scene: "In the waiting room"

Three families sit waiting to be seen one afternoon in a Child and Adolescent Mental Health Service. One of the mothers wears elegant casual clothes and her blonde hair is neatly styled. Nevertheless she looks tired, haggard and ten years older than her 37 years. Her husband is sleek in a dark suit. Occasionally they converse briefly, in low voices. With them is a silent girl, about fourteen. She is wearing baggy trousers and top, but despite this she is noticeably thin. Next to them sits a young black woman flanked by two sad looking boys.

> They both lean against her, one about six, the other a little
> older. She is reading quietly to the younger child. Occasion-
> ally and unobtrusively her eyes fill with tears. Opposite them
> sits a large untidy woman, the buttons of her cardigan strain-
> ing across an ample midriff. Beside her a pallid teenage girl is
> flicking through the pages of a magazine. At her feet is a push-
> chair containing a sleeping toddler whilst two other children,
> five and six, play noisily with the waiting room toys. A further
> boy occupies himself by sliding across the floor on his knees.
> He can make it nearly all the way across the room if he takes a
> run from somewhere over by the entrance door. Every so often
> his mother calls to him to pack it in because he will make holes
> in his trousers.

Each family is made up of individuals, subtle blends of thought
and sensation, spirit and body, emotion and intellect, poised in
their particular stages of physical and social development. Every
individual's existence is embedded in complex inner and outer
worlds, simultaneously creating, and caught in, webs of meaning. Each family is one of these webs, patterned and constantly
evolving in time and space. When systemic psychotherapists
are required to achieve engagements with them, these engagements are at once individual and collective. Their intervention
is both a dramatic performance and a private experience. For
those involved, therapy is private, public and political, all at the
same time.

Meaning-making is central to the therapeutic enterprise. New
understandings and feelings are needed to carry participants
through problematic life situations and challenges. Each family,
each person in the waiting room will encounter the therapist in a
different way, and it is the practitioner's skill to facilitate the creation of new and healing meanings with and between each and all.
For these reasons, working with families is a tough and demanding
task, requiring complex blends of observational and communication
skills. Head and heart have to work together, what we know being
held within the context of what we feel, whilst emotional realities
are recognised and addressed within the framework of knowledge.
The necessary transformations of therapy can only take place in this
multi-level, holistic matrix.

The people in our fictional waiting room may or may not be interested in literature; may or may not, in fact, have the necessary skills or motivation to read more than the front page of their favourite newspaper. Possibly the therapists who meet with them will not have read any imaginative literature for many years, and may not have got much out of it when they did. There may be no one who feels that anything beyond everyday humdrum experience has any personal relevance, yet all of them are preparing, in one way or another, to join in an enterprise of great subtlety and complexity. They cannot help it—this is what therapy is about. It is necessary to find a way to span the gap between the preoccupations of everyday life and the vision of what may be possible. Literature typically fulfils this role, and a literary bridge may offer a path for even the most unlikely of feet.

Carrying on from Bateson

Back in 1967, Gregory Bateson attempted to map a theory of cultural connectedness and the non-verbal arts in his essay "Style, Grace, and Information in Primitive Art" (1972, p. 128). Bateson's thoughts and writings have permeated the development of family therapy, and have appeared and reappeared in theory and practice developments throughout my acquaintance with the field. I would like to focus for a moment on his remarks about poetry. My purpose is to interest fellow therapists in stepping into the domain of literature, in order to facilitate and extend their abilities in just the sort of complex engagement proposed above and needed by our families in the waiting room. Bateson's view is that art is a conscious communication about the nature of underlying unconsciousness and "a sort of play behaviour whose function is ... to practise and make more perfect communication of this kind". Art works are not so much messages from the unconscious as indications of, or comments upon, the relationship of levels of mental process. Poets, he says later in "Form, Substance and Difference" (1972, p. 464), are specifically concerned with the relationship of intellect and emotions, which he defines as levels of mental process. They also build bridges between internal and external aspects of mind, and these are the bridges we use when we engage with arts in general and poetic literature in particular.

At the beginning of the 2000s, theoretical developments in many fields, including that of systemic therapy, have helped us to feel confident in rejecting unhelpful binary distinctions. We now prefer "both … and" to "either … or". This leads us to seek ways of engaging more holistically with our clients, with colleagues, and with aspects of our own lives. We have absorbed Maturana's assertion (1978) that there can be no "instructive interaction" or real power to influence except by a process of co-evolution, and we have accepted that therapists cannot consider themselves separate from the people they work with. The notion of objectivity has been largely banished from the therapy room and from the thought processes of the social sciences researcher. We attempt to co-create realities with our fellow humans, looking for healing narratives and solutions, and we pursue collaborative ways of working. We only feel comfortable when we are not being "expert", and we continue to puzzle over the need to "not know". The "self" of the therapist has moved to centre stage (even if this is a de-centred therapist) and "self-reflexivity" must be shown in all activities. Much of the therapeutic task is performed in the head and through talking, but therapists, clients and service commissioners also desire behavioural change and evidence that interventions are effective.

Narratives

The move to a narrative mode has been one of the major shifts visible in the world of family therapy and systemic practice. Many therapists now operate within a metaphor which enables them to use the imaginative power of personal and shared stories. This therapy addresses the relationship between people and the narratives which surround and shape the ways in which they, and we, see and are seen. The importance of narrative forms in making sense of experience can hardly be overestimated. Narratives are seen as the means to "plot our passage across time and enable us to offer to ourselves and to others some explanation of how we have become who we are" (Dallos, 1997, p. 64). They are excellent and, it might be said, our dominant examples of "patterns which connect" (Bateson, 1988, p. 11). Lives, and events in them, may be simultaneously composed of an infinite multiplicity of such narratives, some of them harmonious but many of them contradictory and conflicting. They are social constructions, and as such are dependent on both authors and audiences for their generation and interpretation (see Chapter Six).

Much has been written about the implications of the narrative metaphor in such disciplines as psychology (Bruner, 1986, 1990; Dallos, 1997), qualitative research (Shotter & Gergen, 1993; Lieblich et al, 1998), psychotherapy (McLeod, 1997), medicine (Greenhalgh & Hurwitz, 1998; Charon, 2006), narrative therapy (White & Epston, 1990; White, 2007), and work with children and families (Vetere & Dowling, 2005) and in the area of attachment narratives (Dallos, 2007). It is a rich and extensive field, of which this is just a taster and an opportunity to "signpost" some useful texts.

From a more literary point of view, the narrative may be seen as but one manifestation of what we might find between the covers of a book. It is the "telling of an event", and in most cases the putting of events in an order and timescale which makes sense of them. As we shall see later (Chapter Four), literary narratives and their narrators are not always what they seem, and can mislead and manipulate. This ensures that the reader has to work quite hard to find a position for him- or herself in relation to what is presented. In this way, literary narratives are distillations of the flawed and indeterminate stories of "real life". Many other aspects of literary texts impact upon the reader: the choice and ordering of words; the evocation of associations and emotional responses; physical and mental images; states of arousal which are stimulated by the sound and the forms of language. Sometimes, as in a poem like Ezra Pound's "In a Station of the Metro" (Chapter Three), the image is foremost and the narrative, if there is one, must be generated by the reader or readers from a combination of their own resources and the suggestions which come from the poem itself.

Novels usually tell a story of some sort, so a narrative thread usually weaves through the fabric. In his book *Aspects of the Novel*, E.M. Forster (the man who exhorted us to "only connect" in his novel *Howards End*) emphasises the importance of the relationship between the narrative and the stuff of everyday life. The story on its own "is the lowest and simplest of literary organisms". When it succeeds in connecting what he calls "the life in time and the life by values" (Forster, 1927, pp. 42–43), and also keeps the reader wondering what happens next, the result is the rich and complicated organism we call the novel. This description is not so different from what we would expect narrative thinkers and practitioners to give today. If we want to look more carefully at how written narratives can inter-relate with lived narratives (and readers who have got thus far probably do want to), we need to consider the metaphorical capacity of literary readings to interact with everyday lived experience (see Chapter Three) to make meaning. We may also want to look at emerging relationships between the "literary mind" and others which may feel more familiar: the "scientific", the "practical" and the "rational" mind (Turner, 1996).

However "real" any of the narratives we encounter seem to be, either in the consulting room or between the covers of a book, we need to remain sceptical about their capacity to pin down meaning. We live in language and are empowered by it, but we are also its prisoners. American novelist Toni Morrison said in her 1993 Nobel Prize lecture: "The vitality of language lies in its ability to limn the actual, imagined and possible lives of its speakers, readers, writers. Although its poise is sometimes in displacing experience it is not a substitute for it. It arcs toward the place where meaning may lie."

A range of resources

Using literary resources includes an interest in and valuing of nar-ratives both great and small, but it does not imply either a method of therapy or a limitation of literary matters to narrative alone. The lad in the waiting room who is intent on polishing the floor with his knees may be prepared to be engaged therapeutically in a great vari-ety of ways, but the suggestion here is that a liaison with the adven-turousness of *Treasure Island*'s Jim Hawkins, the magic of Harry Potter or the worldly wisdom of Bart Simpson may encourage him towards transforming his accustomed realities into something pre-ferred. A therapist whose consciousness has also been stretched may engage with him in a particularly apposite manner.

Let's look for a moment into the therapy room of the service we visited in our initial vignette:

> The therapist is a woman, elegantly dressed, with a slight remi-niscence for a hippy youth in the long earrings she is wearing. She has worked with families for more years than she cares to remember. She welcomes the family into the room and ensures

that they are comfortable. This is the second session. Mrs X, the lady with the tight cardigan, barely touches the chair before she starts to complain about her eldest son. Her daughter picks listlessly at a couple of threads which are hanging off the bottom of her jacket and stares out of the window. The five- and six-year-olds continue to occupy themselves. Everyone ignores the little person in the pushchair, who is still asleep. The son in question sits slumped in his chair. His jacket is zipped up to conceal the lower part of his face and his hood covers the rest.

Several starts on the conversation fail to interrupt Mrs X effectively. Something in the demeanour of our lad sparks the curiosity of the therapist.

"Tell me, (boy's name), what do you like to do when you have the choice?"

Fortunately he does not reply with the name of a computer game, of which the therapist knows little (although she would improvise). He likes to watch TV and prefers horror films. Does he ever read anything? "No." His sister now falls about laughing and his mother begins to look interested.

The therapist searches her store of horror movies—what particularly has he enjoyed recently? He recently saw *Dreamcatcher* and watched it with his mum.

The therapist wonders which was his favourite bit—she knew there was a lot of rather deadly farting, but what else? He liked the bit where one of the characters escaped in the snow. What was good about that? Did he (the hero) make it? What was it like for the others left behind? How did they deal with their fear and their disgust? etc. The therapist is reluctant to settle for a "dunno" answer, and actually she receives few of them now that her young client is talking about something which interests him and he has chosen to speak about. Furthermore, he is now engaged in talking about a film, which opens another world of possibilities, albeit rather gorily expressed. There is in this fiction a horrible situation which requires desperate measures. There is a friendship system which enables some characters to survive against all the odds, and when others succumb, there is the option to reflect on their predicament. There are monsters and conspiracies—all easily translatable into the world of an unhappy adolescent. Above all there is a world which is different from normal, an imaginative landscape in which escapes and solutions are possible.

This fiction also engages his mother and gives them a common focus of attention. The sister has something she can join in with or reject—perhaps naming something else in its place.

We will leave them to finish the session with a new set of concerns and an emotional connection to the problem at hand. The therapist does not need to spell out the connection—it will be obvious from the way the talk has developed, and can be left inexplicit for the time being.

Poets, therapists, poetry and prose

Few psychotherapists have been attracted into their profession because they crave clarity and simplicity. If only others would let them, like John Keats (1817) describing his notion of "Negative Capability", most would relish "being in uncertainties, mysteries, doubts". They would happily forego "irritable reaching after fact and reason" in the interests of profounder understanding. It is no coincidence that this poet's definition of a state of openness and readiness fits for many psychotherapists. Both poets and psychotherapists are pursuing the transformation of complex human experience through the operations of language. Like the wedding guest who is compelled to attend to the story of Coleridge's Ancient Mariner, the psychotherapist is drawn to witnessing unknown tales of terror, fury and misery in the hope of discerning and nurturing some potential for transcendence in the depth of the mystery. There will be those, of course, who do not subscribe to this view, but they are probably not reading this book.

Bateson argued that both poetry and prose reflect "the complex layering of consciousness and unconsciousness" which make up what he, after Pascal, calls "the reasons of the heart" (Bateson, 1972, p. 138). Poetry is not, he maintains, "a sort of distorted and decorated prose" but rather prose is "poetry which has been stripped down and pinned to a Procrustean bed of logic" (*ibid.*, pp. 134–136). Like Robert Frost, who says: "Poetry is what is lost in translation. It is also what is lost in interpretation" (Frost, 1964), he maintains that this multi-layeredness, and the close relationship with the "reasoning of the heart", makes it impossible to translate art works, including literary texts, into forms other than those in which they were originally presented. The changes inherent in interpretation and translation would destroy both the content and the quality of the "information" they embody. In "Style, Grace, and Information in Primitive Art", Bateson recalls Isadora Duncan's famous saying "If I could tell you what it meant, there would be no point in dancing it" (1972, p. 137). For our purposes this means that the text itself, particular words in a particular order, and also, perhaps, in a particular type or binding (see Chapter Five), conveys something fundamental that is inexpressible in another form or through interpretation.

Reading—engaging with the "other"

T.S. Eliot suggests that literary writing represents an escape from emotion and the confines of the personality (Eliot, 1920). If this is so, how can it relate to the everyday concerns which we expect to encounter in our therapy practices? The focus of this book is on a purposive reading of literature. I suggest that this kind of reading puts us in a frame of mind which is expansive and marries up the emotions with the intellect, not allowing either to dominate but obliging them to work together. Transcendence of the status quo is at the heart of the matter, enabling readers to construct new realities on their own, because they are always interacting with what is being read, or in conversation with others. Each reading is a fresh version of what is written, deeply and inevitably affected by the relationships, systems both greater and smaller, of which the reader is a part. It is something which the reader does with the text, prompted by what comes from within, by the circumstances of the reading, and by what the writer has set down. This process has been considered by reading theorists, as we shall see in Chapter Two.

My reading of Eliot's "escape from personality" suggests that poetry, and literature more generally, obliges us to step outside our own thoughts and feelings and engage with the "other": people, ideas, patterns of experience which are beyond our current repertoire. Otherness may even include aspects of ourselves with which we feel less familiar or comfortable. In reading we have to follow a train of thought and an elaboration of response which is external to our personal experience. We have to process it using our own resources. Literary reading offers the material and imposes the conditions necessary for practising engagement with the "other". In our therapeutic work we are always seeking to make connections with other people, be they clients or colleagues. Sensitivity to difference is a vital skill for helping professionals. External appearances may suggest that the people we meet are more or less like ourselves. Experience suggests, however, that personal identity and cultural definitions may be as various as the individuals they pertain to.

Where interventions are being made into the lives of individuals and families, professionals need to be ready and able to recognise and respond to each unique set of circumstances, rather than operate on assumptions arising from previous encounters (Burns & Kemps, 2002). Otherwise there is the danger that we objectify other people and circumstances, failing to acknowledge our responsibilities and our own part in constructing new patterns. This is a particular ethical problem for helping professionals, who must always be on their guard against misuses of the power inherent in their roles. Active reading of literature, as we are defining it, is a kind of antidote to thoughtless assumptions. It obliges us to supply the energy to make personal sense of what we read. By going a little further, noticing the slant of our meaning-making tendencies and making conscious efforts to develop them in particular ways, we move towards nurturing a critical faculty for the reader and a reflexive stance for the therapist. Offering people in less powerful positions the opportunity to find a focus for discussion in a medium of their choice is one way of beginning to redress an unequal balance.

Families in the waiting room

So what literary inspirations precisely might be called upon to assist the helping professional to engage with the people who are in our fictional waiting room? To do justice to this question we need to start quite a long way back and enquire what kinds of reading might help anyone to an active appreciation of, and willingness to engage with, the "otherness" of human life. The answer here is probably any reading which takes us beyond our own experience, sparks our interest and ignites our curiosity. This process can begin with the very earliest experiences of reading and being read to or told stories.

In a study I did a few years ago, I talked to family therapists about childhood reading and asked what they thought might have lasting significance. They mentioned a great variety of reading matter from fairy stories, myths and legends through Anne of Green Gables to Enid Blyton's Famous Five. The latter were mentioned by each of the senior family therapists who participated in my study. What these books supplied were accounts of lifestyles and activities which were at the same time recognisable and excitingly different. Who were these exotic creatures with endless time and opportunity for adventures and minimal adult supervision? The Famous Five were children in some ways like ourselves but in other ways quite fantastically free to follow whatever whim came upon them. Normal social constraints—money worries, or having to go to school, come in on time or account for actions—seemed irrelevant. The series of narratives, however banal, formulaic and politically incorrect, held the promise of a world subtly but significantly different from our own. There was even the opportunity to interrogate gender roles and gender ambiguity if you had a mind to. George was a thoroughly enviable tomboy! You could discuss them with your friends and cross them off a list as you read them. You could re-enact situations, alone or with others, and imagine yourself part of the story. You could dislike the characters and disapprove of them whilst envying their privileges and their ability to find exciting things to do—and all from the comfort of your own chair, floor, bed, or other favourite reading place. Harry Potter's success reflects a similar scene for contemporary children.

I suggest that such early reading nurtures an interactive tendency and fuels its development with a supply of engaging but relatively trivial material to practise with. This process goes alongside, and arguably may even form part of, the web of attachments we build up as a foundation and template for our social relationships. Whilst comforting familiarity is undeniably part of its appeal, imaginative literature of any sort issues an invitation to curiosity. Even Milly-Molly-Mandy, a memory from my early life and surely the most repetitive of all literary characters, prompted interesting questions. Why, for example, do children enjoy (and their adult readers tolerate) having to hear a list of Milly-Molly-Mandy's immediate family every time she takes an action of any sort? I was a keen consumer of these stories in my preschool years and was disconcerted, many years later, to spot in this story the possible genesis of my enduring fascination with the family and my eventual career.

Literary reading is based upon the notion of interaction between reader and text, and much modern and post-modern writing is very explicit in what contribution it demands from the reader. It is difficult to read Virginia Woolf, for example, if you insist that everything be laid out for you. Such writers as Toni Morrison and Margaret Atwood positively drag the reader into the interstices of their novels, leaving no choice but to be an active participant in the generation of meaning. Many critics (and therapists) would maintain that this all started in English with Shakespeare (Cox & Theilgaard, 1994; Bloom, 1998), who combined dramatic narratives with language full of images which were all the more striking because of their contradictions and indistinctness (Carey, 2005). "Whodunits" have always relied to some extent on the active participation of the reader as problem solver. Such contemporary crime writers as P.D. James employ an additional range of literary devices (including the creation of a particular emotional tone, often by powerful evocation of a sense of place) to ensure that the reader remains hooked and actively involved. Clearly, then, there are plenty of places to start deliberately developing the openness of "negative capability" and extending a relational repertoire with the help of literary texts.

Literary inspirations for therapeutic conversations

Given an initial predisposition to curious engagement with the other, on what literary works might a therapist have practised, consciously or unconsciously, with "topics of the trade" in mind? How many other literary inspirations might find a useful place in therapeutic conversations? What connects with whom, and in what way, is always an individual matter, hence the difficulty in having a supply of ready-made therapeutic literary "prescriptions". One size does not fit all. There is also the question of finding something which can create and/or strengthen links between the participants under the unique conditions of a particular therapeutic conversation. In my experience, this can rarely be planned; it needs to arise directly out of the conversation of the day. Therapists who have been following up on the idea that literature may provide other useful voices in therapy should have confidence in the intuitions which they begin to have as to what text or quotation might fit with a particular set of circumstances. Naturally, any ideas the therapist has will be introduced tentatively, in the spirit of a joint project to be entered into as a kind of experiment. This leaves space for ideas to come from all sides. Nevertheless, some recommendations may be useful, and training sessions are more easily structured around selected literary texts.

Parents and children

The following suggestions are personally, but really quite randomly chosen. They are disparate and range from extremely tragic to hilarious. Relationships between parents and children can be explored through the legends of Abraham and Isaac or Ishmael in the Bible, Torah and Koran, not forgetting Wilfred Owen's searing variation on this theme "The Parable of the Old Man and the Young"; the Ancient Greek legends of Oedipus; Shakespeare's plays *Romeo and Juliet, King Lear* and *Hamlet*; Stella Gibbons' *Cold Comfort Farm*; George Eliot's *The Mill on the Floss*; Arthur Miller's *All my Sons*; Kahlil Gibran's *The Prophet*. Pascale Petit's collection of poems *The Zoo Father* is very provocative of discussion, especially where sexual abuse and parental mental illness are issues. Many of Seamus Heaney's poems (notably "Digging", which is featured in the next chapter) concern relationships between generations and the different modes of self-expression over time. Virginia Woolf's reflective novel *To the Lighthouse* is a memorial to, and exorcism of, her dead parents, and a meditation upon the passage of time. It is wise to be flexible about the definition of literary medium and include TV, film and video—almost any episode of *The Simpsons* has something to say about parents and children. In the early days of my family therapy training, the TV series *Dallas* provided endless extreme examples. Currently it is unwise to dismiss *EastEnders* as a source of social relationship models.

In the helping professions there is no substitute for careful listening by a practitioner who is both sympathetic and empathetic, someone who appreciates the situation in the context of the larger systems which surround it, and someone who understands to the greatest possible extent from the inside too. This understanding comes from a stock of personal experiences. The balance of sympathy and empathy available varies over the therapist's life and exposure to life events. A true balance of these predispositions enables the therapist, doctor or other professional to recognise the limits of what they know. There is, of course, a sense in which no-one can fully know the experience of another (Maturana & Varela, 1980; Carey, 2005) or the solutions for their problems, and it is for this reason that specific stances of "not knowing" have been developed in therapeutic theory and practice. These help therapists appreciate the value and truthfulness of not knowing the answer to the conundrums of life which are brought to them. How could anyone else "know" the bereavement experience of the mother and her two children in our waiting room? They may not appreciate each other's, and this may be why they have sought professional help. We'll meet them again in Chapter Seven.

Here is where the natural externalisation of talking about a literary example may be useful. The meaning of "externalisation" here is anchored in a specific composed text. For example: "Here is what this story says and how it says it—maybe it means something for you, and maybe by focusing on it we can have some ideas or feelings which may help us to move forward." This is particularly so when there is a written text, maybe with additional visual images. Literary potential for externalisation may facilitate links between family members as well as between clients and therapists. It may be argued that parents and their children always exist to some extent in separate cultures, and a willingness to attend to each other's formative influences is very helpful in bringing them together. Literature lends itself particularly to this because it is language-based, and whilst people can be divided by a common language, more often (and given the will) the spoken and written word can bring them together. This use of "externalisation" sits comfortably beside the general principle advanced in narrative approaches to therapy, which is that it is useful to see people as separate from their problems (White & Epston, 1990).

Useful books of "therapeutic stories" are available (Bowen & Robinson, 1998), although the idea is advanced here that most story books are capable of therapeutic reading. Some come highly recommended for specific situations. *Badger's Parting Gift* and *Charlotte's Web* are often suggested for children facing the death of a loved person, but what about *The Lovely Bones* and Stephen King's *The Body* (which appears also as the film *Stand by Me*) for those who are seeking ways of exploring their grief for lost children and continuing to live through the process? The Antigone of Sophocles provides a powerful discussion of the impact, in personal and wider systems, of the death of an adult sibling, and Charlotte Bronte's *Jane Eyre* contemplates a range of personal losses and resilience in the face of deprivation. *Fugitive Pieces*, a poetic novel by Canadian poet Anne Michaels, takes the exploration of abandonment and loss to new depths. If we are looking to a broader canvas to contemplate social exclusion and what happens to people and relationships when whole groups are displaced, disempowered and disenfranchised, then John Steinbeck might be our man. *The Grapes of Wrath* remains a powerful testament to suffering at both the macro and the micro level.

It may be a mistake to try and select texts which can inform us about the world of a child or young person whose intimate allegiances may be concealed from the observer: far better to ask the person concerned. In the absence of a comprehensible answer, however, we could perhaps consult Holden Caulfield, the famous disaffected young person in J.D. Salinger's *Catcher in the Rye*. Mark Haddon's recent *Curious Incident of the Dog in the Night Time* gave its readers a precious glimpse of the constraints and possibilities of a world where people and things constantly surprise. Here the protagonist handles language (and is handled by it) in strikingly unfamiliar ways.

We may also have to travel into areas which feel very unfamiliar or uncomfortable to us. Many young people only play computer games and/or read horror fiction. Sometimes they have a taste for music, and lyrics are available to be talked about. Stephen King's writing can offer some common ground, as his work ranges from the seriously literary to the satisfyingly unacceptable "gross out", e.g. the *Dreamcatcher* sequence earlier in this chapter.

Conclusion

We have begun to look at some of the theoretical and practical reasons for introducing arts-based approaches, and literary reading in particular, into therapeutic work. Benefits may come both through the training and development of therapists themselves and from the use of literary resources directly in clinical work.

This chapter contains pointers and prompts. I am drawing on what I know and what has been introduced to me by others, and that is mostly in English. What works for whom in the huge field of the world's literatures remains to be explored. Without doubt, many people the world over are using literature at this moment as a route to knowledge, understanding and healing. Each encounter is unique, and each expedition into the unknown is likely to bring back something of value.

Exercise: Head and heart

CHAPTER TWO

Practising with literature

A scene: "Up in the air"

"How's it going?"

I am standing at the coffee table with some trainees who are attending the second academic block of their Master's level part-time training in family therapy. We are just about to begin our personal/professional development group. They are talking in twos and threes. Most seem relaxed enough, but one or two look tired and a little edgy. I have asked them to bring a "literary" extract, a poem, a short piece of prose—anything which has caught their attention in the interval between the last meeting and this. The idea is to allow the extract to lend eloquence and to provide a springboard for reflections on the trainees' progress on the course.

"Just wait till you hear my poem!" says one woman. "That'll tell you how it's going!"

She was right. As she began to read aloud from Wendy Cope's poem, we began to understand just how she was feeling:

I am a poet.
I am very fond of bananas.

> I am bananas.
> I am very fond of a poet.
> I am a poet of bananas.
> I am very fond.
> A fond poet of: "I am, I am"—
> Very bananas.
> Fond of "Am I bananas?
> Am I?"—a very poet.
> Bananas of a poet!
> Am I fond? Am I very?
> Poet bananas! I am.
> I am fond of a "very".
> I am of very fond bananas.
> Am I a poet?
>
>   —Wendy Cope, "The Uncertainty of the Poet"

The words tumble past each other, patterns forming, dissolving and re-forming. Images hover before the mind's eye. Expectations rise, mutate, and slip away in surprising directions.

As the seven group members begin to get to know each other, they are intrigued by the poem as a witty conundrum and pleased with its polished word play. Initially they find it light and a little bit childish—which is a relief for them, as the first few weeks of the course have left them feeling battered and, in fact, slightly infantile. The experience of trying to fit complex academic learning alongside accelerating clinical development has rendered them apprehensive and exhausted—and the course has only just begun.

One thing is comforting, though. The words of the poem help each person individually to feel that they are not alone: "just substitute the word 'therapist' for poet and it's really me!"

The form of the poem, how it sounds and what it looks like on the page, provides a common focus, something everyone can share equally, if they choose. There's no need to expose our own vulnerability just yet, while everything is still so new. There's a poet who is prepared to do that for us.

Just look at how the words are put together: all the first six lines begin "I am", but in the seventh the poet seems to notice what is happening and how madly self-conscious and absorbed this sounds: "I am, I am", bananas in fact! The last lines are much more questioning. Everything has been thrown up in the air and comes down in a jumble of ideas and language. In the end the question is: "Am I a poet?" or, for us: "Can I become a therapist?"

But there's more still. "I am" remains a powerful statement. The proclamation shouts from the page and hangs in the air of our group room. We feel it speak to us, to teachers and to learners alike. It addresses us all, as participants in the therapeutic enterprise, in our private as well as our public lives. Some people in the group feel crushed by the weight of expectation at the outset of two years of training. The proclamation "I am" is there for them, with or without those "bananas" they are so fond of.

But wait a minute. What does "fond" actually mean here? Does it just mean liking something? Isn't there a sense of foolishness, even madness? Doesn't Shakespeare's tragic hero King Lear call himself a "very foolish fond old man" (*King Lear*, Act 4 scene 7) as he recognises he is not in his "perfect mind"? Maybe the poem appeals because it helps us to say we are not feeling quite in our right minds, or that our minds are changing in ways which feel chaotic.

Once we start to look beyond the poem itself, having seen there is meaning in it for us, we feel the unaccustomed excitement of following our own intuition. Familiar boundaries blast away into imaginative space. As someone has made a link with King Lear and the suffering he goes through to see things clearly at last, so another thinks of a juggler who is performing for an audience and trying to keep as many balls in the air as possible. Isn't that one of the reasons some people feel on edge? They are always on show during this training. Clinical work is recorded on video. There is a viva voce exam and seemingly endless assessment. Clients, colleagues and course staff make up a demanding audience. How can we get through without dropping some of the balls?

But wait a minute. Isn't there another way of looking at it? Just as the poet juggles all those combinations of words and syntax publicly, and risks losing it to get something across, maybe we have to learn to be consciously self-conscious, to try to see ourselves as others see us, so that we can perform our chosen therapeutic functions?

And what about this other idea—that everything is "up in the air", disintegrating to make space for new integration? The motion is whirling, dizzying, rather like eddies of water, catching and holding leaves and twigs from the river bank, then letting them go to float downstream. On this stream of association we move on to the next literary fragment, *The Whirlpool*, a novel by Canadian writer Jane Urquhart, which questions our relationship with fluidity and force in learning and in therapy. Suspended thus in water, the students feel the strength of their desire to make something of this learning experience mixing and merging with the fear of possible failure.

Postscript

That morning we moved through a landscape of associations, some familiar, some new. What we didn't realise then is that Cope's poem shares a title with a painting by Giorgio De Chirico, "The Uncertainty of the Poet". The painting accounts for, but does not, of course, explain the reference to bananas. The rich web of contemporary associations for the word "bananas" may have looked rather different in 1913, when the painting was produced.

The picture might have led us more directly to reflect on the aspect of psychotherapy training which is to do with seeing, being seen and, because family therapists typically work with groups, being seen to be seen. Family therapists already make this partly explicit through the traditional manipulation of space and visibility which comes with using a one-way screen. We would perhaps have debated the importance or otherwise of trying to achieve coherence whilst balancing all kinds of inconsistencies, discontinuities and even absurdities in therapeutic interactions with people and situations. The picture shows a twisting female torso: no arms, hands or legs. We might have reflected on the traditionally seated therapist in the midst of a family group, twisting round in an effort to include all members, using words rather than hands and mind games rather than physical ones. Since the torso also lacks a head, we would be forced into considering just how those words could be produced and what kind of thinking would be possible. There could be nothing proceeding from the traditional source, the brain inside the skull. No chance of speaking in the traditional way. De Chirico's picture also includes a big bunch of bananas, and the whole is set in a perplexing landscape, absolutely begging to be considered in the light of contemporary contexts for practice.

The vignette group has been busily engaged in what might be called reflective reading. Members first selected little snippets of text which had caught their eye since the previous session. Sometimes their search for extracts resonant with their current experience took them back to a poem or novel they remembered from the past. Occasionally a participant, thinking of themselves as not "literary" in any way, chose to bring a picture, an object, a song or a story they felt connected to. In the session, participants presented in turn what they had brought, explaining how it connected with their current preoccupations and then inviting others to share their responses. It was a bonus to have extracts read aloud, because the sound of the words on the air brings the whole thing alive. Incidentally, a surprising number of otherwise competent and confident people feel uncomfortable with reading to others, a discomfort mostly ascribed to humiliating childhood experiences at school. It is worth trying to encourage everyone to read aloud, and given the encouragement and safe environment of the group, the fun of sharing and playing with spoken and written words can be a revelation.

In sharing their responses, group members were constructing new realities, following paths they would have had no way of discovering on their own, and establishing a common pool of ideas and images. This process is especially productive because literature is our living repository of ideas and images, from the "wordhord" of Old English (*Beowulf*, l. 259) to the "pool where we—and in this case by we I mean the vast company of readers and writers—go down to drink and cast our nets" which features in Stephen King's novel *Lisey's Story* (2006). And this is just English literature.

Literature—why bother?

Now we have reached the moment to pause and unpack some general ideas about literature and the point of engaging with it. In his useful online notes for literature students, Professor John Lye gives a number of suggestions as to how literature might be said to work (http://www.brocku.ca/english/jlye/uses.html). These suggestions mirror quite precisely the points which a number of senior British family therapists made about their own relationship with literary reading, first in a Delphi study and subsequently in interviews (Burns, 2003). I am drawing on both these sources in the bullet points below. Literature:

- explores the texture and meaning of human experience, using forms and methods which develop insight and rich reflection concerning our lives and the nature of human experience.
- creates "possible worlds", imagined dramatic constructions of experience which allow the artist to explore basic "rules" of human nature and of the structure of the world.
- operates through a process of "mimesis", re-presenting reality so that it can both be experienced directly and also perceived as artifice. We are drawn by aesthetic devices into the reality of the experience, but are simultaneously distanced from it so that we can reflect and theorise about it.
- creates defined imaginative worlds, using cultural codes (systems of signs which establish meanings and relationships) with more density, subtlety and complexity than other communication modes. This is a characteristic of art in general. Arguably, therefore, literature lends itself more easily to reflection than immediate experience does, prompting us to be more conscious of our cultural environment, more alert to meanings, more flexible and more analytic. In this way, literary texts can be "more real than reality" (see below: "What has this got to do with therapy?" and Chapter Three).
- gives us the language with which to talk and think about our experience. Using the language of literature gives a fresh perspective and locates personal experience within a cultural frame.
- uses language precisely and effectively. Engaging with literature helps refine our capacity to use language and develop sensitivity to effective language use. The ability to conceptualise, analyse and to express—maybe even to experience—emotion is dependent on the ability to use language. The quality of internal conversations we have with ourselves is also dependent upon the sophistication of our use of language.

- models and examines "subject positions" (socially constructed roles like "mother", "father", "child", "therapist", "client", etc.) and allows us to enter imaginatively into positions we might not otherwise occupy. Literature also allows a critical examination of the nature and integration of the subject positions we do occupy, thereby promoting a sense of self which is more able to respond to the possibilities and limitations arising from our physical and social contexts.
- exemplifies the world view of the writer and his or her social/political context. Because of literature's imaginative and expressive power, reading can be a very effective way of engaging with particular cultures in their own time and space. Conversely, the choice of reading material and how it is used can reveal much about the culture and values of the community of readers.

Before we leave the question of what busy people, whether therapists or just plain folks, might gain from reading some poems or novels, I want to add the simple thought that literature gives pleasure. Everyone needs pleasurable activities to leaven the heavier and more indigestible aspects of life. Therapists in particular have to attend to this need, not only for their personal protection but also to give them the option of lightening up their own therapeutic style. Therapeutic change needs to be gratifying if it is to be effective, and it is a mistake to underestimate the practical value of pleasure for all participants in therapy.

What counts as "literature"?

For many of us there is a vague implication that "literary" refers to writing which is designed for an elite audience, is difficult to consume, and requires prior knowledge and a high level of literacy. This implication is certainly real. Bookshops and libraries may categorise their wares in such a way that "literature" is segregated from "popular" or genre fiction (like "romance", "crime", "science fiction"), and "classics" are often in a section of their own. The notion of a "canon" of texts is a powerful one. These are texts which are thought appropriate to be taught in schools and universities. The existence of a canon also implies that certain groups or individuals are in a position to define what should be read (and also, of course, what it is worthwhile to write). Fortunately, canonical questions do not need to distract us here, except in so far as we all need to be able to find the texts that other people want to talk with us about, i.e. they need to be in print or available in some other way. However, just as the unprecedented accessibility of information on the internet is revolutionising the relationship between healthcare professionals and the public, so it is changing the ways we think of texts we might want to read for their own sake. John Carey says: "literature is writing that I want to remember—not for its content alone ... but for itself" (2005). Many such texts are now available through internet archives such as Project Gutenberg and university-maintained web pages such as Voice of the Shuttle (University of California, Santa Barbara). Some books are published online.

Literary criticism and theory form a massive body of work which overlaps in places with the kind of theory which has informed family therapists and systemic practitioners in recent years. For example, Jacques Derrida, Michel Foucault and Ludwig Wittgenstein all find a place in the Johns Hopkins Guide to Literary Theory and Criticism (Groden et al, 2005), along with big sections on feminist criticism and poststructuralism. This should not surprise us, as both family therapy and literary criticism are language-based disciplines which share many theoretical assumptions and questions.

"Literature" is used throughout this book to mean writing (primarily) which we value because of the connection it makes with us through its content and its form: what it says and how it says it. The nature of the connection is important. This needs to be multi-layered so that our emotions are engaged as well as our thoughts, because this combination is what provides the energy for us to elaborate and improvise around what we have taken in—to open up possibilities and feed our creativity.

Building bridges

Gregory Bateson asserted that artists and poets are concerned with building bridges between different levels of mental process (Bateson, 1972, p. 464) and that art is a communication about the patterns of our lives. My own relationship with four literary texts exemplifies this. When I was writing up my study of family therapists' reading, I recognised the importance of contextualising my own part in the enquiry and set out to write a reflexive commentary. One of the texts was "The Lady of Shalott", another was Virginia Woolf's *To the Lighthouse*; hence the part these texts play in this book. The former is a poem by the Victorian poet Tennyson in which the Lady of the title is confined, by threat of a curse, to "Four grey walls, and four grey towers" on an island, where she weaves a tapestry which depicts the world as reflected in a mirror. I thought this poem described in a metaphorical way the feeling of oppression I felt when I went to university to study English. It connected with my experience on many levels, and helped me to reflect on how my feelings, understandings and motivations at a certain point in time influenced the course of my life, turning me away from literature and language study and towards the social sciences.

The poem set out a living dilemma: stay safe on the island and weave the tapestry or look to the outside world and risk the curse. I mapped this onto my own experience and found the comparison immensely informative. As a technique of writing up research findings, the reflexive commentary gave structure and added meaning. As an example of guided reflection, it provided a template for clinical and personal/professional development uses. The literary "bridges", I discovered, depended less for their significance on the story than on the feel of the poem's or the novel's particular world. The link was an experiential one. Only a part of my external life was ever like that of the Lady of Shalott, and our developmental paths diverged dramatically. What spoke to me was the way in which the elements of the poem came together, its ambiguous and slightly spooky atmosphere, its romantic medievalism and its implicit comment on women's positions.

So what does count?

Let's now return to the question of what counts as "literature". Given a definition of literature which highlights the creative nature of our connection with it, we can go on to include not only written texts but all sorts of words and pictures which invite or allow interpretative responses, where emotions and imagination are at the forefront, with a view to the transformation of meaning. The way is open for the reader both to experience and to interpret. The definition of what counts as "literary" resides with the "reader", who selects from what is available, using his or her own motivations and capacity to make new sense of, and in, the world. It is a subjective process involving interaction with an external object (text) and other subjects (writer, other readers, etc). Hence, in the formal setting of a personal/professional development group for trainee therapists, the participant who brought a commemorative plate as a focus of personal reflection, and the others who wanted to talk about a football match all made valid use of the "literary" aspects of their choices. Literary texts, novels, plays and poems give us a magnificent start, with language and ideas already composed to facilitate or demand reflection. Written texts are my starting point, and I would argue that a poem or a piece of a novel gives us more to work with, but the same potential exists in many other cultural artefacts. What counts is the connection the person feels to the object, and the significance it has for them. It would be a mistake to be confined by an exclusive definition of literariness.

Reader response

This way of looking at reading as a creative social and cultural activity has been the business of "reader response theorists" for several decades. These thinkers propose that meaning is not located in the text or in the reader, but in the relationship of reader and text. The most notable of these, for our purposes, is Wolfgang Iser.

Iser considers the reading process in great detail (1974, 1978), defining it as a joint project involving the activity of the reader guided by the text. He also outlines the relationship between literary texts and what might commonly be called "reality". For him, literature is a form of cultural discourse, having functions within the culture as a whole (1989). He maintains that literature always complements dominant patterns of thought and action: "We might say that literature answers the questions arising out of the system ... the literary work implicitly draws an outline of the prevailing system by explicitly shading in the area all around that system" (1978, p. 73). It can therefore be a force for cultural integration. The respondents to my research questions pointed out firmly, however, that it is also a form of discourse which can be controlled to some extent by an elite. It may therefore also lend itself to the maintenance of power in the hands of select groups. This is a danger, especially for therapists who are in a position to exert substantial influence over vulnerable people (however they choose to limit this power), and must be kept constantly in mind and subject to review.

As for the individual's relationship with what he or she reads, Iser proposes that meaning is generated by an interaction between reader and text that ultimately transcends both and belongs exclusively to neither. This happens because the indeterminacies in a text ("holes" in the narrative, unanswered questions, etc.) oblige the reader to do the creative work of drawing together the actual and the possible, to open up the potential in what is read and in the act of reading. In other words, the reader has to use his or her own experience to fill in gaps, both in the work itself and between the work and the reader's perception of everyday reality. This follows in a long tradition, beginning in the ancient world, of seeing engagement with literature as a source of self-realisation.

The meanings generated by the reader in relation to a text are felt emotionally as well as understood intellectually. This is linked with the notion that literary works do not just tell us about things, they perform what they are about. The poet William Wordsworth not only tells us that Westminster Bridge is a fine place to be in the early morning, because of the beauty of the scene and all the reflections it prompts, but the words that he writes also give us the feeling of being there and experiencing the accompanying thoughts and sensations at first hand:

> This City now doth, like a garment, wear
> The beauty of the morning; silent, bare,
> Ships, towers, domes, theatres, and temples lie
> Open unto the fields, and to the sky;
> All bright and glittering in the smokeless air.
> —Wordsworth, "Composed upon Westminster Bridge,
> September 3, 1802"

The writer, therefore, supplies words capable of conveying and generating emotional intensity and meaning. The reader brings his or her own experiences, ideas and existing emotional repertoire to bear, and the result is a joint production. The approach explored in this book does not demand that the reader admire (or even like) the work in question. We are not talking about appreciating an art work. We cannot be forced by a text into a particular type of response, although we can be ardently wooed and persuaded!

Iser's work is theoretical, but some reader response theorists in his tradition have gone on to take a more empirical approach. Some actually study readers whilst they are reading, using a variety of methods including self report commentaries (Miall & Kuiken, 1995). They put increasing emphasis on the feelings involved in reading literature (Miall & Kuiken, 2002), shifting the focus from textual interpretation to highlight the role of the emotions in reading and of reading in the development of self. This shifts us towards seeing literary reading as a tool for developing that fundamental social skill, the individual's ability to imagine and respond empathically to the states of mind of other people, sometimes known as theory of mind. This view opposes any idea of literature and its consumption as an optional extra, a kind of embellishment of ordinary life.

What has this got to do with therapy?

We left the group at the outset of the chapter enjoying shared reflections on their own training experience. This may be all very well, but how does it transfer into their forthcoming lives as therapists? Why have we picked on poems and novels as particularly relevant to psychotherapy practice, and the activity of reading as worth writing a book about for systemic practitioners?

This approach took shape for me over two or three years following my qualification as a family therapist. This was a time when I decided to revisit previous aspects of my life and interests. It was a sort of consolidation period in which I felt the need to reconcile current passions with previous ones. When I had safely achieved a therapy qualification and begun to practise, I enrolled in some literature classes and again fell under the spell. Having manoeuvred myself into this position, I then began to find a thought creeping in with increasing urgency: "this critical reading is just like the sort of thinking and talking I do when I'm working with families, only better". By this, I meant that it felt more deeply rooted in me as a person, and more meaningful both to me and, I thought, to others. Both reading and therapy involve a critical, but appreciative, dialogical engagement with a chunk of language, on the one hand a written, sung or spoken text and on the other a therapeutic conversation which is itself a "virtual" text. Transformation is the aim. Of course, reading and therapy differ in many ways, but they had sufficient significant features in common to grab my attention and make me curious about what ideas and practices might emerge from a closer juxtaposition. The idea never went away, and is the basis of what is between the covers of this book.

That therapy and literature share a special relationship is not just a preoccupation of mine, however, so let's look at the proposition more closely. Bateson, as we already know, thought that the delineation and exploration of the relationship of different levels of mental process was the business of poets as much as, if not more than therapists (Bateson, 1972, p. 464). Bruner followed along this route, maintaining that literature as art sensitises us to dilemmas and possibilities such as are inherent in therapeutic processes. Moreover, he says, it is a source of "freedom, lightness, imagination, and, yes, reason". It is "our only hope against the long gray night" (Bruner, 1986, p. 159). Both literature and therapy have at their core a process of social interaction and meaning-making mediated through text/ conversation which is transformative of experience, both individual and shared.

Michael White, drawing on Bruner's work and also on Iser's, explores the "text analogy" in relation to the ascription of meaning in human life as well as in reading. He concludes that good stories are generally more transformative of meaning than poor stories, and sets a reading and discussing exercise for students seeking to learn more about the structure of good stories and the importance of literary merit in therapeutic discourse (White, 1992, pp. 82, 91).

In their book *Pragmatics of Human Communication*, Watzlawick et al use Edward Albee's play *Who's Afraid of Virginia Woolf?* as a method of presenting interactional communication which they say is "possibly even more real than reality" (Watzlawick et al, 1967, p. 150). The focus of this "super reality" is the interdependence of individual and environment. Playwrights and therapists are both preoccupied with exploring this interdependence. They both enable participants, viewers, readers, therapists and clients to arrive at a different, enhanced apprehension of their particular slice of "reality", i.e. play or therapy session, along with its context. Anderson and Goolishian (1988) describe therapeutic interchanges as linguistic affairs where problems create systems of actors and meanings, which transform themselves and are dissolved in turn through the purposive use of language. The same may be said of a Shakespeare play, the Cope poem at the top of this chapter, the 19th century novel *Wuthering Heights*, or an experimental modernist novel like Virginia Woolf's *To the Lighthouse*.

Literature and therapy, then, have been quite widely seen as similar activities. The participants in my research, however, would not settle for this rather too neat analogy. "Literature does not have healing as its primary purpose," they said. "Therapy does not have to satisfy aesthetic demands." And of course they were right. The idea here is not to reduce one activity to the other, but instead to see what mutual enrichment can take place.

Digging for victory?

To conclude the chapter we'll eavesdrop on a different group of trainees. This time the students are divided into two groups. One group has a copy of "Digging" by Seamus Heaney (1966/2006) and the other "A Parcel of Land" by Pascale Petit (2001). For a moment the group members look puzzled. "What's she up to now?" they wonder.

> We had been discussing how new training first dis-integrates the trainees' sense of self and then re-integrates it in order to move forward. We have considered how painful this can be, how hard it is to hang on to what is valuable from the past whilst being open to what we need to take on for the future. The topic is very similar to that preoccupying the group at the top of the chapter, but different because it is a later time with a new group. I ask them to read the poem they have—someone in each group volunteers to read it aloud for the others—and then to think about how the poet is addressing the question they are preoccupied with. One poem, "Digging", speaks of how the skills of one generation or time are handed on to the next. The tools and circumstances are different but the spirit of the activity is the same. One generation makes its way with a spade, the next with a pen, but continuity is precious. The other poem is also about passing on an inheritance. Here there is a play on words: two kinds of "parcel". The groups sit in two circles, leaning in towards each other, absorbed with the poem they have before them and how it whispers to them of shared hopes and fears.

When I get home, I notice Homer Simpson on my Christmas present mouse mat. Here I see yet another variation on the theme of disintegration, reintegration and handing on what is precious. He is clutching the top of his skull and yelling silently: "Every time I learn something new it pushes some old stuff out of my brain!"

"Very true," I say to myself.

Exercise: Enriching therapeutic discourse

CHAPTER THREE

Living with metaphor

"All the world's a stage,
And all the men and women merely players;"
(William Shakespeare, *As You Like It*, Act 2 Scene 7)

A vignette

The scene is the family therapy suite in a community mental health service. On this occasion the room contains just two women. They are discussing the aftermath of a particularly painful relationship breakdown. "The trouble is," says one (we'll call her Sue), "I keep getting into really bizarre situations with men. It's as though I really can't resist a man other people find unacceptable. It's been a pattern with me for years and it's taken all my confidence. I can't understand it. I just go round and round in circles."

At this moment a light bulb comes on in the head of the other (yes, she is the therapist). "Have you ever read *Wuthering Heights*, the novel by Emily Bronte?" she asks. "I only mention it because it just popped into my head as you were talking.

There's something in that story which reminds me of what you're saying: something about still wanting to walk on the wild side, even if you can see it's no good for you."

...

The same room a couple of months later. Again, just the two women are present. Sue speaks: "You know you kind of suggested I looked at *Wuthering Heights*? Well, I tried. I really did. I thought it would fit in OK with the work I've been doing for the OU [Open University] Humanities course. I couldn't stand it though. All that wandering on the moors and over the top dramatic stuff? What nonsense! Anyway, for some reason I'm feeling a lot better about myself. That kind of thing just isn't for me, you know."

Another vignette

A group of family therapy trainees is grappling with the question of what register of voice and language is serviceable in talking with client families. One group member had become uncomfortably conscious, when speaking in the therapy room, of the choices to be made. A client had remarked that she, as therapist, was "talking posh". She was appalled, because this was directly opposed to her ideas of how to "be" as a family therapist. She came from a long and honourable line of helping professionals, for whom overt emphasis, say through style of speech, on social differences between helper and client would be at best unhelpful and at worst unethical.

This group was using literary extracts to facilitate their Personal/Professional Development (PPD) group. An extract from Alan Bennett's *Writing Home* came along just in time to provide a focus for discussion of this dilemma. The extract revolved around an incident in which Bennett's mother had seen, but not recognised, T.S. Eliot in the street. She had merely seen a distinguished-looking man, apparently not from Leeds, wearing a smart overcoat and accompanying a local woman. Mrs Bennett had not recognised him for very good reasons. She and he did not move in the same social circles. Son painstakingly described to mother the significance of Eliot in the great scheme of things: he had won the Nobel Prize, after all, to which mother immediately replied: "I'm not surprised. It was a beautiful overcoat" (Bennett, 1994, p. x). Group members seized enthusiastically on Bennett's analysis of different registers of speech, and their relationship in his own writing.

We did not find a solution to the language question that day, but our attention was firmly nailed to it by means of this little story. Group members were grateful for a lead in confronting their own issues. Most of all, they enjoyed sharing "Eliot's overcoat" as a peg to hang their reflections on!

I have given these two vignettes to illustrate a couple of important things about metaphor. The first shows how engaging with a story so that it speaks about another situation, at an emotional as well as an intellectual level, can help to shift a predicament which has proved resistant to other sorts of remedies. This is the essence of metaphor: that one thing is described in terms of something else which is literally distinct and dissimilar, e.g. "our family is a mine-field". Even in everyday use it is a striking and economical device. The attributes of the "minefield" (state of war, need for extreme care and minute observation, fear of serious injury, dangerousness of relaxation, etc.) are used implicitly to amplify the meaning of "the family". In the previous chapter we discussed the kind of engage-ment with literary texts that involves the reader generating his or her own meaning and significance, guided and stimulated by the texts. By the way, "text" here means not only the stories but also all the other linguistic features of poems, novels and so on. Sue, the woman in the first vignette, was aware of the dangers of her yearn-ing attachment to a certain sort of partner. She was motivated, intel-ligent, and had plenty of evidence to indicate that she should avoid such relationships. All the same, she was stuck—that is, until she suddenly "knew" that this way of doing things was not for her: she was just not that kind of woman!

Wuthering Heights

This novel relates the tale of Catherine Earnshaw, a passionate woman irresistibly drawn into a destructive love relationship with the wild outsider, Heathcliff. She simply cannot leave the relationship alone even when it threatens her life. In the vignette, the therapist thought she could see parallels between this and her client's story in terms of mood, emotional atmosphere and a superficial correspondence in some narrative elements. Curious as to what Sue would make of the novel, she mentioned it. *Wuthering Heights* is generally accepted to be an emotionally provocative read. The effect is achieved, amongst other things, through the imaginative construction of an inclusive world in which extreme emotional intensity is the norm. Readers may love it or hate it, but are rarely left unmoved.

In this instance, a remarkable personal change is related casually during the next session. It is mentioned almost in passing, despite the fact that trying to achieve it was the main focus of previous therapeutic conversation. This change is taken at face value, and no attempt made to ascribe it to anything in particular other than good sense. Sufficient to say, the client had got as far as experiencing the Heathcliff/Cathy impasse for herself, through a preliminary sampling of the novel, and had felt a strong reaction away from it. One explanation for her potentially life-saving change of heart is that she not only felt the pain but was also able to stand outside it, fully feeling a strong aversive reaction and making it her own (see also *Literature—why bother?* in Chapter Two). In this way she found the story of Cathy and Heathcliff a powerfully involving metaphorical communication about her own situation. The significance of her adverse reaction reminds us that we are not in the business of literary appreciation here. Although there will often be an element of admiring a work of art, what really matters is the active involvement of the reader's responses. Of course there were undoubtedly many other factors involved in Sue's achievement. By her own account, however, the juxtaposition of the reading "assignment" and the difference in view of self speaks volumes.

"A beautiful overcoat"

In the second vignette, T.S. Eliot's overcoat has a different kind of metaphorical significance. It is the receptacle of ideas and feelings about a complex interactional phenomenon—the social use of language. The group seizes on its symbolic significance and uses it as a focus for conceptual and emotional elaboration. Alan Bennett himself describes the story as "a kind of parable" and links it with his own use of "two different voices" (1994, p. xi). "T.S. Eliot's overcoat" also assumes importance as a "shorthand" term which conveys the richness of the discussion, the experience of being part of it and the life of the group, as in: "Remember T.S. Eliot's overcoat? That was a good morning's discussion." When I subsequently analysed the transcriptions of the group's sessions as part of my research, it became clear that metaphorical images such as "the whirlpool", "mountaineering", and "T.S. Eliot's overcoat" had a powerfully organising effect on subsequent conversations. This effect was not always consciously noticed by participants. They were merely impressed by the fact that the group seemed to have developed the ability to think and feel together, even without having to make much conscious effort to do so. We will talk more later on about the power of mental images. For now, let's look in more detail at some views of metaphor.

Metaphors we live by

In their book *Metaphors We Live By*, Lakoff and Johnson (1980) maintain that all our language is infused with metaphor whether we are aware of it or not. Sometimes we do not recognise the metaphorical nature of common expressions like "getting on top of" paperwork, the ironing, our fitness programme; or of the reverse, the paperwork getting on top of us. Things "get us down", and we may feel "down" if we are "depressed", which is also metaphorical, by the way. Some metaphors are so "entrenched" (there's yet another) in our "use" of language that they are called "dead". "Understand" is a good example of this. Most of us would not see this word as having much metaphorical significance, and its figurative origins only appear when we consult an etymological dictionary. Once we begin to look for this "infiltration" of our everyday talk by metaphor, we can find it everywhere.

The metaphors we choose exert a powerful influence upon the way we look at the world. They shape the ways in which our communications are received. It can make a great deal of difference, for example, for a parent experiencing difficulty with an errant child to express a wish to "get through" the situation, as opposed to "get round" it or "get it sorted", even though all these are common expressions used in the resolution of interpersonal difficulties. The very idea that disagreement can be "resolved" (this is a word I often use in an effort to be more neutral and avoid the meaning load of other phrases) also carries with it the implication that there has been some individual or collective error of perception. It suggests that there is, at the least, a muddle that needs clarifying, and that someone (or everyone) needs an improved focus and a more analytical approach. This is what it suggests to me when I take the time to think about it. There is, of course, no "correct" interpretation of common metaphors, and it is wise for professional language users like therapists to be aware of a range of possible "understandings".

We do have the option to make conscious choices about the metaphors we use, however, and we can critically appraise the metaphors we accept. In his book *Metaphors of Family Systems Theory*, Paul Rosenblatt (1994) explores the "standard" metaphors of family therapy as used by therapy practitioners, researchers and theorists. His focus is on metaphors for "the family" rather than metaphors for "family therapy". This is a challenging and refreshing approach, beginning with a critical look at "the family" when it is seen as an "entity". Rosenblatt reminds us that when we adopt one metaphor, however relevant and enlightening, there is the danger that it will blind us to the relevance and usefulness of other metaphors. So the adoption of "family as entity" metaphor may imply the dominance of "the family" over individual members. It carries with it the danger of superimposing a spurious coherence on a group of people who also diverge and differ. Other metaphors like "family as a system", "family as a structure", and "intra- and extra-family interaction as communication" are explored, with the effect of de-familiarising these old friends and encouraging a critical re-evaluation of common assumptions. None of this suggests that one metaphor is more or less "true" or helpful than another, but it certainly highlights the importance of therapists' awareness of the language they use and its implications.

Metaphors that lead us on

When we consciously select the metaphor which we think will help our cause, we may find that it will take us further, and have more far-reaching consequences than we expected. If we, as therapists, adopt the metaphor "conversation" for what happens in the therapy room, we may find ourselves acting, thinking and positioning ourselves very differently from when we are predominantly concerned with something called "intervention", which is a more active, instrumental and non-collaborative metaphor. It is likely that both metaphors have to be held in balance to satisfy demands arising from the context of practice. In a public agency, for example, "interventions" are likely to be funded and "conversations" are not. Therapeutic practice metaphors operate not only for direct participants but also in the minds of those who construct the context, our managers and the commissioners of our services.

Although Rosenblatt specifically excludes the study of family therapy as a system, readers might want to reflect for themselves on the relative implications of metaphorical descriptions such as "therapy as strategy", "therapy as co-evolution", "therapy as narrative", or even "therapy as reading". Consider also something like the "circle" in "circularity", "circular questioning", and so on, or the loop in "feedback loop". Are these circles and loops more like mechanical circuitry in our minds' eyes, or are they lazy meanders in the delta of a great river? Do they play the same tune endlessly or take us on train journeys, either under or over the ground? Can we be tortured upon them like King Lear?

> but I am bound
> Upon a wheel of fire, that mine own tears
> Do scald like molten lead.
> —Shakespeare, *King Lear*, Act 4 Scene 7

Getting the right metaphor can make a big difference in all sorts of activities. For example, in her chapter on qualitative design, Valerie Janesick (1998) applies the metaphor of dance to the stages and demands of the research process. The design she describes is a type of choreography, and its stages mirror the warm-up, exercises and cooling down which the dancer needs in order to perform his or her art. Discussion of meaning in research follows the questions and debates of dance. When I came upon this approach as I looked for ways through my own research, I found it inspirational because she had managed to import both perspective and relevance into hers in a uniquely meaningful way. This doesn't mean we all have to get interested in dance, but it did teach me that to find the metaphor which speaks personally can be the key to enquiry, be it clinical, research, or personal/professional development, which has real originality and startling relevance. We'll look at this a little more in the next chapter.

Metaphors and thinking

Metaphor analysts like Lakoff and his colleagues have further concluded that metaphor is the chief component of concept formation and building. "Far from being merely a matter of words, metaphor is a matter of thought—all kinds of thought ... It is indispensable not only to our imagination but also to our reason." As a common tool which we all use every day, it "allows us to understand our selves and our world in ways that no other mode of thought can" (Lakoff & Turner, 1989). By this token, then, metaphor is a pretty powerful and pervasive force, enabling us to generate new thoughts and to elaborate them in conversation with others. Even so, we tend not to notice that it is happening, hence the surprise for the family therapy trainees, who suddenly became conscious of communicating together with amazing immediacy and effectiveness through the medium of something so irrelevant (in a literal sense) as "Eliot's overcoat" or "mountaineering" (see Chapter Five).

Neuroscience is rapidly building pictures of the interrelationship between body, mind and environment. We now have the technology to see what happens in our brains when we engage in various activities. In his 2003 Reith lecture, V.S. Ramachandran proposed that the phenomenon of synaesthesia (a neurological condition in which two kinds of bodily sensation are coupled, e.g. numbers or letters are perceived as inherently coloured) could be explored in order to give "an experimental foothold for understanding more elusive aspects of the mind, such as what is a metaphor" (www.bbc.co.uk/radio4/reith2003). The body becomes more closely and demonstrably implicated in our ability not only to feel but to think (Damasio, 1999). These developments are important for us as readers and therapists because they encourage us to keep worrying away at the idea that something as elusive, yet as common as metaphor is crucially important in our work.

Why literary metaphor?

Given that so much consideration has already been accorded to everyday metaphor, what does the literary angle lend to the discussion? Metaphor, it seems, is basic to our language, to our ability to experience and to our capacity to communicate adequately about it. Generic metaphors give shape and direction to our actions.

Common tools, however, can achieve dramatic effects in the hands of gifted craftsmen and women. Literary writing is an art form as well as a means of communication. It has meaning and value in and of itself because of the form of its expression. This meaning supplements whatever serviceable information is conveyed. It gives added value. This is what we heard from Watzlawick in Chapter Two, when he says that literature (in this case Edward Albee's play *Who's Afraid of Virginia Woolf?*) presents us with a heightened and refined version of human life which is "more real than reality" (1967, p. 150). This refinement and expansion is achieved via the craft of the writer, in conjunction with the meaning-making capacity of the reader. Literary texts also carry cultural meanings and significance. The investment in literary metaphor is amplified through the commitment of writers, readers and their communities. Literary metaphor's capacity to stimulate creativity and reflection is, therefore, proportionately greater and richer.

The deliberate choosing and elaboration of metaphors from poems, songs, novels and plays have a specific contribution to make to the way we build concepts and respond to situations. With this in mind we move the discussion of metaphor onto a different plane. When Shakespeare says "There's daggers in men's smiles" (*Macbeth*, Act 2 Scene 3), we know that there's treachery afoot, that men who smile are not to be trusted, may in fact be murderers, and that therefore life can never be the same again. As we develop our thinking through this metaphor, a web of associations, which is potentially infinite, begins to form itself around our perception. Most important of all, we feel something of what it is to be in this predicament. The precise nature of our feelings will depend on what we bring of our own experience. Even though we are not Macbeth, we are likely to look, for the moment, more suspiciously at our environment to see if we can spot the danger, or catch sight of any daggers in our companions' eyes!

There are only a few examples in family therapy literature of therapists using literary examples to inform therapeutic conversations. Dallos and Trelfa do just this in their article "To Be or Not To Be: Family Beliefs, Madness and the Construction of Choice" (1993). In this example, therapists grapple, alongside a troubled family, with how they define and are defined by their relationships in the context of wider societal discourses. For the family in question, an impasse has developed between parents and an adult son, with mutual mistrust and recriminations. The therapists are keen to explore what choices are available to family members and what might enable them to make the most of their creative potential, both individual and shared. Since the family is of a literary persuasion, they all find themselves discussing *Hamlet*. The choice of this text arises directly from the family, in response to a suggestion from the therapists that they make a conscious effort to divide their family interactions between business and pleasure. Going to the theatre together has traditionally been part of this family's "fun". Both therapists and family in this particular situation are preoccupied with the meaning and implications of "madness", in both intimate and broader systems, so *Hamlet* seems to be an excellent choice.

Shakespeare's brooding tragedy gives structure and impetus to the exchange of ideas, but no-one seems to be under the impression that they are doing anything else but confronting their own predicament. They find themselves exploring the "essence" of the play, in which an agony of indecisive "not knowing" gives rise to a sequence of disastrous consequences. Family members envision themselves on this particular stage and they discuss whether or not real life can be more controllable than the overtly scripted drama. To what extent is it possible to write the script of our own lives as we go along, and what choices are there?

This is a good example of the power of a literary text to mediate the generation of new perceptions and feelings, as well as to provide a helpful externalisation of painful and contentious interactions. I hope the authors will forgive me if I make some improvisations on their theme. How would it have been, for example, if this family and the therapists had attended a performance together, or had even got further "inside" the metaphor by reading part of the play together?

It might be thought that this kind of activity needs approaching with care, as in the play *Hamlet* almost all the main characters wind up dead. Thinking about dramas like this one in relation to personal circumstances would indeed be risky if people could not distinguish between what happens in a play and what happens in lived everyday life. It's important to be able to say "it's only a story", and it may be argued that many societal ills could be ascribed to their proponents' inability to tell the difference. Drama therapist Sue Jennings proposes that we hold in mind at least two realities: the everyday and the dramatic. In her view "maturation is the capacity to distinguish everyday and dramatic reality and to be able to move in and out of each appropriately" (1998, p. 117). In this case, a new focus for therapy might have emerged in which parents and son, with the help of the therapists and the play *Hamlet*, could have experimented with sorting the dramatic from the every-day—which of their interactions belonged where? This might have involved closer engagement with the "dramatic", represented by the play, to clarify that certain of the family's thoughts, feelings and real life behaviours might actually sit more safely within the "dramatic". "Drama" is a common metaphor for therapy, as it is for family life. In this metaphorical context, therapists and clients are permitted to move freely between roles. Available parts include the dramatis personae (cast list), and also the functions of direc-tor, stage manager, front of house, producer and audience, from the front stalls to "the Gods" (cheap seats at the very back of the circle).

Mental images

The trainees at the beginning of this chapter were part of a research group and had the rare experience of having their sessions recorded, transcribed and given back to them for their comments. This meant that reflections were cumulative, and feedback from earlier sessions could be incorporated in later ones. I had the privilege of analysing the transcripts and seeing the vital part played in the group proc-ess by the images contained in the literary extracts brought by the members. I say "images" because these vivid sensory happenings in the mind seemed to carry the burden of what we have already called metaphorical communication. These were images like the whirlpool, the juggler, climbers on the mountainside, a field in which running figures converge (the first chapter of Ian McEwan's *Enduring Love*), and—more abstract but equally evocative—the "starting point" which we come back to and "know it for the first time" (T.S. Eliot, "Little Gidding, 1942"). In one session, the image of a colleague's imagined funeral came to dominate the scene and then to galvanise group members into action to support each other. The feelings asso-ciated with these experiences are essential to their effect.

In the experience of this group, "image" and "practice" are in a circular, mutually connected and enriching loop. The interaction between the two is mediated in language through the action of metaphor and the discussion of the group. In another sort of book this might be represented via a stylised "circle" or possibly a hierarchical arrangement of little loops between levels of context. This would make a lot of sense and help with the visualisation of the idea. The trouble is, now that we have raised the question above, which of the many kinds of circle or loop might we envisage? We have to clarify the options. Will a plain "powerpoint" kind of loop do, or should we go for a more fluid, discursive or decorated kind of thing? Maybe a Celtic knot, or a serpent devouring its own tail? Each different image would generate its own webs and pathways of significance, so it will make all the difference.

The influential American poet and critic Ezra Pound says: "An 'Image' is that which presents an intellectual and emotional complex in an instant of time" (1913). Early in his career, Pound was one of the prime movers in the poetic "Imagist" movement. This was a group devoted to the production of succinct verse which was clear and precise, and in which the poetic statement was delivered entirely through the use of a clear visual image. There was, in their adoption of this austere discipline, a wish to move away from the vagueness and perceived verbosity of Romantic and Victorian poetry. Pound's poem "In a Station of the Metro" (1977) presents the image of individual faces against the surrounding darkness of the crowd in the Paris underground:

> The apparition of these faces in the crowd;
> Petals on a wet, black bough.

The image is stark, and the image is all there is. Whatever meaning the reader takes from it depends upon very few words, but its impact is powerful and emotionally compelling. The faces in the poem float against a background which is devoid of light and detail. Or is it beautifully gleaming and fragrant with the smell of damp foliage? Maybe the faces are a little like faces in the singular environment of a therapy room? What, after all, do we pick up in situations where we are distracted, either by our own thoughts or our own anxieties? How do details of our environment enter our consciousness and what do we make of them? What does either therapist or client take away from a therapy session? My experience suggests that there will be a lot of information to write down and make sense of, a narrative of the session if you like, but there will also be an emotional atmosphere which is instantly recreated through a particular image or series of images. We may talk about them, and they are regenerated with varying degrees of vividness in our own language, but basically they are more about pictures in the mind's eye than about words.

Thinking about images is in some ways the antithesis of what we have explored above in relation to metaphor. Images come straight at us and speak directly to the depths of our being. Thinking about them comes next. As Gaston Bachelard, philosopher of science, puts it: "But the image has touched the depths before it stirs the surface" (1969). Images defy, or precede, the narrative explanations which we might apply to the metaphors discussed above. The reader response theorist Iser and the philosopher Bachelard agree that literary or imaginative reading consists mainly in the movement of quickly changing images. Readers must decide for themselves how much this mirrors their experience of therapy. For me, a therapeutic conversation consists of an outward and predominantly intellectual exchange of ideas and explanations. There is also the manipulation of conventional social activities like greeting and giving people seats, finding out how they are, and exchanging various kinds of information. Alongside all this, in my mind at least, there is a succession of mental images. These images are strongly metaphorical and they may be more or less abstract, hovering somewhere between the outward appearances of people and analogies which arise from my experiential repertoire. They might include, as they did with a family I saw yesterday:

- small 14-year-old lad, flip-flopping between two images:
  - young male robin, piping loudly, offering to do battle with any and every challenger who might venture into his territory; or
  - hyped-up but battle-weary gladiator unable to give up the fight because his life depends upon it;
- mother as relentless "kindness machine": in the nicest and most proper way a bit like the erotic torture device in the 1968 science fiction film *Barbarella*;
- father as mischievous gnome, kindly intentioned but never fully committing himself;
- older sister as "patience on a monument", as my grandmother and, incidentally, Shakespeare used to say (*Twelfth Night*, Act 2 Scene 4, l. 113);

• whole family, and therapist, slumped listlessly about like the contents of a turned-out toy cupboard, or the rag dolls in Beatrix Potter's story *The Tale of Two Bad Mice*, who looked on at all the chaos and made no remark.

All of these visions and sensations were momentary, fleeting, telling no coherent story but creating a powerful atmosphere both during and after the session. We are not accustomed to owning up to these kinds of mental images, and it is by no means clear what part they play in shaping the activity of therapy. Even so, we might concur with Bachelard, suspecting that images are as influential as, if not more than, ideas. If this is the case we should take care to note them so that we can learn to use them in the service of our work.

The family above will continue trying to make sense of their situation, with me as therapist. The images in my mind will power my part in our conversations and enter into the "text" we create. In this, I am drawn to Bachelard's observation that "an imaginary life—the true life—begins around a pure literary image" (1988, p. 30). The last image in my list was a literary one: the speechless dolls from Beatrix Potter's story *Two Bad Mice*. Starting with this image and guided by the text, I arrive at a couple of pages from the book's end where the little girl, the owner of the dolls' house now ransacked by the two bad mice, intervenes. She has a practical solution: "I will get a doll dressed like a policeman!" she says. The family in my example, if they were minded to, might draw some implications from this for their own actions. These might coincide with what the therapist feels might be helpful, i.e. that the authority in the family needs to be strengthened, if not by a doll dressed as a policeman, or even a real policeman, then by the parents acting together. A real policeman (or more likely a judge) is certainly a possibility in the family's future if things do not change and our cheeky little "robin" does not start to attend school more reliably. However, the nurse in the story has a better idea. She says: "I will set a mouse trap."

The mouse trap

There is a simple postscript to this chapter. It has been all about metaphor and how our minds can be led along unknown but productive routes, if we have the courage to let go of habits we rely on.

We know that there are theorists who believe that metaphor is the key to concept building. We know also that the choice of metaphor has a profound effect on how we approach and carry through the tasks we undertake. Thinking about images takes us a step further into the unknown. They invite us to throw over our accepted disciplines and pursue something much freer. Sue, at the head of this chapter, had only to glimpse the image of Catherine Earnshaw on the wild Yorkshire moors to know that the whole "Heathcliff" thing was not for her. Like her, we can venture, if we have the courage, to take our lead from mental pictures which depart from coherent narrative and lead us to places previously unknown in our everyday consciousness.

So where does the mouse trap feature? A later chapter is going to explore writing as a reflective activity and will be considering how we bring it together with reading to aid our understanding of personal and interpersonal processes. I began this chapter intending only to explore metaphor and use examples from my experience as they occurred to me. It is only now that I see a connection between some of the metaphors and images I have chosen. The nurse in *The Tale of Two Bad Mice* introduces a resource from outside the story's internal frame of reference. Hamlet brings in the party of travelling players to perform a "play within a play" at the Castle of Elsinore, with a view to flushing out the guilty King Claudius to confess to his crimes. This play is called "The Mouse Trap". In this way grows the web of associations which informs our reading and our therapy practice.

Exercise: Pick a metaphor

PART II

TRAVELLING ON

CHAPTER FOUR

Becoming a therapist: putting theory into practice and practice into theory

Vignette: Getting started—not as easy as it sounds!

A young woman sits staring at a computer screen. We'll call her Abigail. She is a primary mental health worker, newly appointed to a community Child and Adolescent Mental Health Service. In Abi's case, this means that she is at the beginning of her career. She would like to achieve a formal qualification in a therapeutic discipline, and has recently completed an intermediate level course in family therapy. Currently she is pausing to consolidate her practical experience.

This afternoon she is trying to make sense of a clinical session in which she tried (unsuccessfully, she feels) to offer help to a troubled adolescent and her family. On the computer screen is a half written document detailing the session. The family in question was not one of those commonly considered "hard to engage". No ASBOs (anti-social behaviour orders) here; no social exclusion or poverty, either absolute or relative, and no lack of education. Both parents are very successful professionals, a senior civil servant and a lawyer, who live with their three children in the best part of town. Even the children made our therapist feel naïve and ignorant. Worst of all, Abi feels she has tacitly concurred with a view that the second child, a painfully angry, self-harming 13-year-old, could be considered a serious rival to head-rotating Regan in *The Exorcist*! The pull to join in the general blaming of the adolescent for the family crisis was tremendous, but Abi thinks she succeeded in retaining some professional distance. She just wasn't able to make any difference to the session's punishing air of negativity and misery. She fears she has actually played a part in encouraging it to develop.

Now the therapy room is empty, she can reflect on the sorry mess she has witnessed. Usually, writing up her session puts things into perspective. She can put her ideas in order and work out how to go forward. Today, however, weaving together her notes is not having the desired effect. Maybe she is not really cut out to be a therapist after all.

***

In another world and another time, a young woman, this time dressed in the style of Arthurian legend, contemplates the ruins of a tapestry in which all the threads have burst from their frame. Close by the loom is a large mirror which has cracked right across the middle. Her weaving seat is placed with its back to the window of the turret room, but she has risen from her chair and turned to gaze into the outside world. The broken mirror still reflects a view through the window, in which can be seen the far off towers of a town and the retreating figure of a rather glamorous looking knight on horseback. He is urging his steed towards what we now realise is Camelot. As he goes, he hums a catchy but inane tune, with a refrain which sounds a bit like "Tirra lirra".

Inside her chamber the young woman prepares to succumb to the curse which she is sure will come upon her, now that the work, into which she has poured her heart and soul, lies in ruins about her feet. [Tennyson, "The Lady of Shalott"]

Vignette: Carrying on—not necessarily a bed of roses either!

Just down the corridor from Abigail, an older woman, Nat, sits in a meeting with her senior colleagues. The discussion has got stuck in reviewing a new approach to assessing and responding to referrals. The method under discussion has some potential benefits, but the attendant form filling is a headache and so extensive that it consumes much time and energy.

Nat is a consultant family therapist, and is therefore a senior member of her profession. She loves her work, especially the large noisy meetings with tempestuous families, which she considers the "heroic" end of psychotherapy. Many of her colleagues would claim this description for their own discipline—which is as it should be, because they are all mistresses (or masters) of their own craft. However, there is a gloomy feeling today amongst the assembled group. Some people feel that the demand for a different approach (even though the previous one worked pretty well) and increased paperwork is really the outward manifestation of more covert and extensive changes. The atmosphere is heavy with suspicion and righteous indignation. This is not just change—they are accustomed to that. This feels like an attack by stealth on their professionalism. Why, the new ways of working may not even be ethical!

Nat is determined to make something of this new situation. She has a pragmatic side to her idealism. It will mean looking deep into the roots of her art (yes, she thinks there is art as well as craft) in order to find the strength and authenticity she needs. Her main tool is herself, and she is not about to allow something essentially trivial to endanger it.

***

Meanwhile, out in the darkness of the bay, a beam of light sweeps regularly across the sea and the land. In the window of a seaside house a woman sits knitting a long sock, which she intends one day to donate to the lighthouse keeper for his son. The stroke of the lighthouse beam provokes in Mrs Ramsay a deep sense of harmony with her environment. She feels at one with the light and with its regular pulse. Losing herself in the experience, she finds a deeper sense of "self", of the limitless potential which lies beneath "all the being and the doing". [Virginia Woolf, *To the Lighthouse*]

Here, then, are two helping professionals confronting potential turning points in their own development. What have two literary characters, the enigmatic Lady of Shalott and the materfamilias Mrs Ramsay, to do with these contemporary transitions? Are they role models? Do their stories illustrate ways to escape from the vicissitudes of personal/professional life? Well, hardly. The Lady is beautiful, reclusive, and at the mercy of an imagined curse. Her example of lying down and dying is not to be followed. Mrs Ramsay, incidentally also beautiful, is an incorrigible social organiser, mother of many, and host of seaside house parties for privileged arty types. Later in the book, she dies distantly, in one line, when all the action has moved elsewhere. Their storylines may be intriguing, but do not in themselves give the inspiration which is looked for here.

What these two characters offer, in my view, is a model of interior processes, metaphors of mind in interaction with environment. Both our therapists are looking for ways forward which seem responsive to the demands of their jobs and also accord with their own personal and professional authenticity. In their different ways these two literary examples provide an articulation of interior conversations, which we now see as an integral part of the therapist's task (Rober, 1999). Mrs Ramsay's character was created with the express purpose of bringing thought processes and feelings onto the page, revealing the interior monologue and making it explicit. Tennyson's Lady, despite her aesthetic values and haunting beauty, goes right ahead and acts out her innermost fears and yearnings to their logical and emotional conclusions.

Literary characters as practical companions in personal/professional development

So exactly how might a few minutes spent with these literary characters help? We'll take the two situations in turn, beginning with resemblances between the "real" and the fictional and going on to consider what inspirations these analogies might offer.

The Lady of Shalott

Abigail is apparently alone with a task which is within her capabilities, providing things go smoothly. The "web" she weaves consists of gathering information and placing it into a frame of theoretical understanding. She knows how to weave this web, where the different colours should go, how the picture which emerges should look. She has been a very good student. If there is a mistake in the weaving, she can recognise it and has a clear idea of what she might do to put it right: maybe ask a certain sort of question, or mobilise some kind of social support. So far, she and the Lady are doing well. Unfortunately, this is a very fragile situation and inherently susceptible to breakdown. Part of the problem is the mirror. For the Lady who "weaveth steadily", the world is represented by the shadows in her mirror. She has, in other words, a theory of the world which she derives from reflections in a piece of glass. On the face of it, this has quite a contemporary feel, fitting as it does with ideas that reality is unknowable except via the lenses or mirrors we use (Hoffman, 1993), and reminding us of the developmental watershed of Lacanian psychology, the "mirror stage" which is the basis of subjectivity (Lacan, 1949). We might accept that "theory" should be good enough anyway, as it is now endless and omnipresent in critical writing and thinking (Culler, 1997). However, as anyone knows who has ever ventured, as a helping professional, to sit with a group of people in high distress, it is what you do and how you do it that counts. Theory is fine when it derives from a combination of imagination and intimate knowledge of the world to which it refers, but not much practical use when it remains abstract.

Since the Lady's web is informed only by the "shadows of the world", there is no challenge to her belief that "A curse is on her if she stay/To look down to Camelot". Abigail is also in danger, because of her limited experience, of becoming imprisoned in the "weaving chamber" of theory. She needs an alternative view, the sort that could come from working alongside a more experienced colleague who knows how theory can become embedded in practice wisdom. This, for her, could be an essential step towards growing personal and professional resilience. In our terms, this would protect her against early burnout.

The next thing that happens in the world of Shalott is an intrusion from the outside world, which is qualitatively different from anything the Lady has previously encountered. Sir Lancelot appears in her mirror, and whereas she has hitherto been content to view passers-by as exterior to her own life, in this case she is drawn to leave her work and look directly out of the window. The result is dramatic:

> She left the web, she left the loom,
> She made three paces through the room,
> She saw the water-lily bloom,
> She saw the helmet and the plume,
> She look'd down to Camelot.
> Out flew the web and floated wide;
> The mirror crack'd from side to side;
> "The curse is come upon me," cried
> The Lady of Shalott.
>
> —Tennyson, "The Lady of Shalott", Part 3

All in an instant, the world of the past is overthrown and there are some serious decisions to be made. There is the option, the reader will probably say in 2008, to abandon the safety of the loom and "get a life", even if it is full of uncertainties and challenges. In the poem, the possibilities represented by the appearance of Sir Lancelot seem to present just too much difference, and she succumbs instead to the dismal, but expected curse. She takes a boat, lays herself out in it and drifts down the river. By the time her craft floats into Camelot she is no more than a lovely corpse.

There are myriad interpretations of this poem, many of them revolving around gender implications and the catastrophic effect of sexual desire on girls who have led sheltered lives. These ideas, though serviceable for many readers in other circumstances, are frankly irrelevant for Abi, who is very satisfied with her gender and her sex life, thank you! What can we see here that may be more helpful to her?

If Abi feels drawn to the mysteries of the Lady of Shalott, if the poem mesmerises her, as it does many people, she will identify with the aspects of the story which "fit". This means an active, but not uncritical engagement with the poem. Such an engagement combines ideas and emotions to extend the individual's repertoire of beliefs, feelings and behaviours. If Abi feels she is potentially entrapped with the Lady, but can also stand outside the action and reflect on it, she is in a strong position for choosing an alternative, transformative "ending" for her own story (a little like Sue in Chapter Three). The metaphorical nature of poetic reality can help her to see the anomaly of behaving like a romantic, medievalist cliché imprisoned in a tower by her own imaginings. She can see the dangers of falling in love with a theory or belief and failing to interweave it with experience. At this level, the poem can act rather like a cautionary tale which says "don't do it like this!" A simple response would be to revisit the question of joint work with an experienced colleague, good supervision, and the support of colleagues.

If we want to go further for a moment, with the Lady as metaphor, we can reflect on the cataclysmic effect of a single moment of change—a casual or reflex action which has unthought-of consequences. We can also recognise the value of a "broken mirror" of theory. There is, after all, a reflected quality in all psychological life, and in our consciousness of "self", and it may be the breaking of the mirror which alerts us to its significance and encourages us to develop it further (Romanyshyn, 2001).

Mrs Ramsay

Mrs Ramsay is another kettle of fish, although "boeuf en daube" might be more fitting, since the family sit down to a particularly delicious one of these during the book. Virginia Woolf wrote *To the Lighthouse* as what we might now call a piece of fictionalised autobiography. In her Introduction to the 1992 Penguin edition, Hermione Lee tells us: "The writing of *To the Lighthouse* was the closest Virginia Woolf came, she says, to undergoing psychoanalysis; she invented her own therapy—the narrative—and exorcised her obsession with both her parents" (p. xxxiv).

In some ways, describing *To the Lighthouse* as autobiography belies its scope and power. It is a full and subtle exploration of personal reality. Each character carries an essential part of the whole (we might call this a distribution of aspects of self), their interactions evoking the muted colours and abstract patterns of a shifting seascape of the mind. Woolf herself rejected the notion that the novel could be read as a series of coded events and that it could be "solved" like a puzzle. In a letter to Roger Fry (1927), she said: "I meant *nothing* by The Lighthouse ... I saw that all sorts of feelings would accrue to this, but I refused to think them out, and trusted that people would make it the deposit of their own emotions."

As we have said, Mrs Ramsay is not advanced here as a role model. She presents, rather, a character whose internal conversations are set forth in exemplary form. It so happens that she shares thoughts and feelings with many women—wives, mothers, carers—who are accustomed to defining themselves in relation to others, who spread themselves thin, and who long to be "herself, by herself ... to think; well not even to think. To be silent; to be alone."

Nat's position is different from Abigail's. She has gone a considerable distance along the road of her professional development. She can absorb whatever most of her client families throw at her and she uses her hard-won skills as a kind of second nature. She is no stranger to the transformations possible as part of a well informed and grounded "talking therapy". She can, and does, offer practical support to the less experienced and resilient among her colleagues, and has useful perspectives on clinical and organisational developments to offer to anyone who cares to ask. As often happens, however, her strengths can easily become weaknesses. She habitually gives out help and support but rarely makes time to ask for it herself. She hates to say "no", and is involved in so much professional committee work that it takes only a small increment for her to become overstretched. Her life is a constant whirl of busy-ness, and she is proud to define herself in terms of her work. It is unusual for her to doubt that she has the "authorised version" of how work in her agency should be organised.

It is not surprising, then, that seemingly trivial changes in referral priorities and their attendant bureaucracy really disturb her. She recognises the interdependence of therapeutic and case management systems, and the prospect of naïve tinkering makes her angry and frustrated. She is not alone amongst her colleagues in giving way to righteous indignation, but she now feels that her reactions are in danger of exceeding her control. Unlike Mrs Ramsay, she is at risk of forgetting how much she needs silence and solitude. In this state of quietude, so elusive and yet so essential, "all the being and the doing, expansive, glittering, vocal, evaporated; and one shrunk, with a sense of solemnity, to being oneself, a wedge-shaped core of darkness, something invisible to others" (Woolf, 1992, p. 69).

Mrs Ramsay needs her "core of darkness" to find resources to deal with the idiosyncratic Mr Ramsay, her children and her house guests. Nat needs hers in order to protect her professional autonomy and authenticity. She is aware how closely intertwined her personal and professional lives have become. They used not to be, but nowadays she can hardly tell the difference between them. This is natural, she thinks, at her time of life, but she also feels in danger of burnout more strongly now than at any other stage. If she were to read *To the Lighthouse*, she would respond at once to other expressions of the "self" described: "this self having shed its attachments was free for the strangest adventures". The outward appearance of the person is maintained as "apparitions, the things you know us by", but "beneath it is all dark, it is all spreading, it is unfathomably deep" (*ibid*).

The "spreading" darkness might sound a little alarming, and for its author, Virginia Woolf, it proved insupportable. Nat is not one to be intimidated by an immersion in darkness, however. In fact, her predilection for the "dark side" has endeared her to many a sullen adolescent. "Better not go too far in that direction!" was feedback she sometimes received from her supervisor. However, a little more distance here, like thinking of the novel rather than herself, would help her get a clearer perspective.

There is at least one more gift which Nat might receive. Mrs Ramsay is very absorbed in, and gratified by, the family and household of which she is the hub. Nat has no children, but she is happy to acknowledge how much she gains from the families and individuals she works with. She also feels a deep connection with some of her colleagues. Far from being a sentimental woman, she can nevertheless find herself profoundly moved by much of the work in which she participates. Something about the current situation has obscured this simple fact. She can give but she can also receive. In fact, the two are indissolubly connected. Like the Ramsay family, ready for dinner and composed into a group by the effects of candlelight in the surrounding darkness, Nat can sit with others in therapeutic sessions and feel part of a whole which is greater than the sum of its parts. This is the token by which her personal and professional self is affirmed.

In the first part of this chapter I have taken time to go into two possible scenes of crisis for a developing therapist, and to take a detailed look at how literary readings might help. This has necessarily been a very partial and limited excursion, and has focused on how a text might offer an external point of reference and a fresh viewpoint on a familiar situation. Learning involves a continuous interaction between thinking and doing, theory and practice. The use of literary examples not only facilitates this process but also anchors it in the emotional life of the learner. Practitioners who have survived a crisis of confidence can go forward to generate new and more robust theory and practice wisdom, either for their own use or for public consumption. This takes emotional energy and commitment.

But these are just dead white females!

I chose the two examples above because they speak to me. I used them to help me reflect when writing up my research into the uses of literature by therapists, so I know they have a lot to offer. This approach seeks to identify and work with subjectivity wherever it has creative potential. Imagine what might come from a similar approach to, say, the narrative reported by Conrad's Marlow in *Heart of Darkness*, Jean "Binta" Breeze's poem "The Arrival of Brighteye", Hanif Kureishi's *The Buddha of Suburbia*, James Joyce's *Ulysses*, Salman Rushdie's *Midnight's Children*, or Stephen King's *The Dark Half*. The suggestions, so far, are modern works in English, because these are what come readily to my mind, but the scope is amplified hugely if we include not only works in other modern languages, but ancient works such as the Old English *Beowulf*, Homer's *Odyssey* and *Iliad* in ancient Greek, the Sanskrit *Ramayana* and *Mahabharata* and even the Sumerian text, the *Epic of Gilgamesh*. My choice would always be to follow the "reasons of the heart" and turn readily to what calls out to the person or people concerned.

Therapeutic training: a task for life

Journals

Journals are traditional companions on life's journeys, and in fact the two words have the same root, emphasising the day-by-day nature of both enterprises. Writing our own journal is uniquely valuable, as we shall discuss in the next chapter, but reading first person accounts of other lives, both great and small, gives us a particularly focused insight and opens up reflections which are distinct from our own. Some, like the Diary of Samuel Pepys, are actual journals, mirroring the life of another place and time. Others, like Daniel Defoe's *Journal of the Plague Year*, are fictionalised accounts of historical events. Some improvise around the trivia of everyday life. Take, for example, the *Diary of a Nobody* by George and Weedon Grossmith, published in 1892. This is a fictional account of the life and daily doings of Charles Pooter, his wife Carrie, their son Lupin, friends Cummings and Gowing, employer Mr Perkupp, and various other inhabitants of late Victorian Holloway. The focus is on humdrum happenings and who says what to whom. By way of introduction, Pooter asserts:

> I have often seen reminiscences of people I have never even heard of, and I fail to see—because I do not happen to be a "Somebody"—why my diary should not be interesting. My only regret is that I did not commence it when I was a youth. [Grossmith & Grossmith, 1892]

Diary of a Nobody reads like a century-early pilot for a reality TV show, with the exception that the Pooters have an ironic edge normally lacking from the likes of *Big Brother*. Much of the family life recounted is instantly recognisable. Here are the Pooters with their son, who has recently (and unexpectedly) returned to live with them:

> I was about to read Lupin a sermon on smoking (which he indulges in violently) and billiards, but he put on his hat and walked out. Carrie then read me a long sermon on the palpable inadvisability of treating Lupin as if he were a mere child. I felt she was somewhat right, so in the evening I offered him a cigar. He seemed pleased, but after a few whiffs said: "This is a good old tup'ny—try one of mine," and he handed me a cigar as long as it was strong, which is saying a good deal. [*ibid.*]

This strikes me as both true to life and funny. It reminds me of the importance of humour in therapy and in personal and professional development. In clinical work it must be a collective phenomenon, arising from the conversation in progress, and not imposed by a therapist. In training, however, humour can be deliberately imported from elsewhere, and its use can be an excellent way of gaining distance from a topic whilst remaining emotionally connected with it. It promotes irreverence as a stance in life, a quality which has been advanced by one of family therapy's favourite gurus as essential for therapists' survival (Cecchin et al, 1991). What is funny is also a matter of individual taste, so it is unwise to assume that what one person finds hilarious will automatically have that effect on others.

Adrian Mole's Diaries are irreverent successors to the *Diary of a Nobody*. They fill the gap left by the youthful Charles Pooter, albeit retrospectively, combining plenty of irony and humour with political commentary. These novels by Sue Townsend now cover a considerable period of time, Adrian Mole having begun at 13¾ and having reached the age of 34 in *Adrian Mole and the Weapons of Mass Destruction*. This makes them ideal companions for the developmental journey of a lifetime, while Helen Fielding's novel *Bridget Jones's Diary* has initiated a looked-for women's perspective on contemporary life, love, and the rightful place of "big knickers" in the female repertoire.

Fiction and "theory of mind"

We have already proposed that a degree of fictionalisation in "real life" accounts adds an extra dimension, in which the author's craft facilitates reflection in the reader. This means that an element of composition has entered the account of events. This element is always present when we reconstruct memories and locate them in a meaningful narrative. Since we are looking to literature to play a specific part in the development of the skills and disposition which are necessary for therapeutic practice, we should perhaps pause here for a moment to look in more detail at what fiction may be said to offer. We are now considering journals, memoirs and first person narratives which are regarded as literature and contain varying and uncertain degrees of fictionalising. Lisa Zunshine's book *Why we Read Fiction: Theory of Mind and the Novel* investigates the field which has been created by the coming together of cognitive psychology (and in particular "theory of mind") with literary criticism and theory. Reading novels, she maintains, is an exercise in "mind reading"—the exploration of states of mind and their attribution to (in this case) fictional characters. "Attributing states of mind is the default way by which we construct and navigate our social environment," she says, "incorrect though our attributions frequently are" (2006). Novels, she says, typically represent the interaction of numerous fictional or fictionalised minds, and so they feed the reader's "representation-hungry complex of cognitive adaptations". The growth of these adaptations is dependent upon "direct interactions with other people or ... imaginary approximation of such interactions", as in works of fiction (*ibid.*, p. 10).

Skilled writers, working within literary traditions, experiment with their readers' "mind reading" capacities and, in the case of such writers as Virginia Woolf, attempt to push them beyond their "zone of comfort" (*ibid.*, p. 37). Literary reading, according to this view, also enables us to acknowledge and examine our own mental processes as they affect the meaning attributions we make (see also *Literature—why bother?* in Chapter Two). I suggest that these are exactly the challenges which we want for ourselves as developing therapists. I often feel that my job as a helping professional is to help others expand and refine their abilities to enter into the experience of others, especially friends, family and immediate social networks. Family therapists particularly focus on this through the use of such techniques as "circular questioning", sometimes even known as "mind reading" questions.

An essential prerequisite of the professional task of encouraging and helping others to "read minds" is that I have also worked on my own abilities in this area, and that I take a position which is as reflexive as possible. This means always asking "what am I bringing to this (therapeutic) conversation?" It is often a labour of love to check out my own abilities using literary resources. The demands of the professional task are easier to meet if there is a similar weighting of interest and excitement. Fiction offers a particularly apposite kind of challenge, but Zunshine is clear that exercises in "theory of mind" are always contextual and may equally happen in other sorts of reflections, such as discussion of a football match (see also *What counts as "literature"?* in Chapter Two).

Memoirs

Memoir is a subset of autobiography based upon memories, and is a subjective take on a person's own lived experience. Such writings often focus on a particular aspect of life. In literary memoirs, like journals, what seems to be important is that they can promote the kind of reflection we are looking for. They must feed and stimulate the impulse that surely characterises the majority of therapists: the insatiable hunger for "reading minds", both our own and other people's. Political diaries (like Tony Benn's or Alan Clark's) can make fascinating reading, especially where they contain liberal helpings of comment and gossip. They are also likely to contain a definite, if indeterminate amount of "fictionalisation". Typically, however, diaries like these present and invite very little self-observation and interrogation, thereby largely failing to encourage a reflexive position in the writer and the reader.

Memoirs are very important for other reasons too. They are eyewitness accounts of historical events, and can be the basis of continuing inspiration for people in the twenty-first century. They invite us to explore "subject positions" which are not our own, and are likely, if we let them, to encourage us to explore our own feelings and thoughts in relation to their content. Again, revisiting *Literature—why bother?* in Chapter Two will help make better sense of this idea.

Take, for example, the American Slave Narratives, an anthology of which can be found at http://xroads.virginia.edu/~hyper/wpa/wpahome.html. These are the verbatim transcripts of interviews given by African American former slaves (1936–38) to writers and journalists under the aegis of the Works Progress Administration of the USA. They give a vivid picture of life in a time of slavery and are a recognisable foundation for the work of writers such as Alice Walker, Maya Angelou and Toni Morrison.

A generation or two earlier, Isabella Baumfree, known as Sojourner Truth, dictated her memoir *The Narrative of Sojourner Truth: A Northern Slave*, which was published privately in 1850. At the Ohio Woman's Rights Covention in Akron, Ohio in 1854, she gave her most famous speech:

> That man over there says that women need to be helped into carriages, and lifted over ditches, and to have the best place everywhere. Nobody ever helps me into carriages, or over mud puddles, or gives me any best place! And ain't I a woman? Look at me! Look at my arm! I have ploughed, and planted, and gathered into barns, and no man could head me! And ain't I a woman? I could work as much and eat as much as a man (when I could get it), and bear the lash as well, and ain't I a woman? I have borne thirteen children and seen most all sold off to slavery, and when I cried out with my mother's grief, none but Jesus heard me, and ain't I woman?

Undoubtedly this speaks with a powerful voice to many people with different allegiances and interests, but it is also an irresistible invitation to "mind reading" in the way we have been talking about. Through this public declamation we can glimpse the personal experience of another human being, in the social context of a time long past, but we can also find our own place in it, whoever we are, and see there the forces and themes which continue to shape our own society.

Formative memories

Memoirs often recall the writer's youth and the influences which have shaped the person. The poet Siegfried Sassoon reflected on his childhood and adolescence, recording them in his *Memoirs of a Fox-Hunting Man*, of which readers are often heard to say "I don't care a bit about fox hunting, but I did enjoy the read!" William Wordsworth also traced and recorded the youthful experiences which shaped his poetical voice in his *Prelude*. In the 1799 (two-part) version he says: "The mind of man is fashioned and built up/Even as a strain of music" (ll. 67–68).

If we seek entry into childhood memories of matchless vividness and intensity, or maybe just want to revisit some of our own, we need look no further than the first part of the 1799 *Prelude*. Here young William, by this time an orphan and enjoying remarkable freedom to wander through the Lakeland countryside, takes a boat and rows out onto a lake by moonlight. His boat is moving across the water like a swan:

> When from behind that rocky steep, till then
> The bound of the horizon, a huge cliff,
> As if with voluntary power instinct,
> Upreared its head. I struck, and struck again,
> And growing still in stature, the huge cliff
> Rose up between me and the stars, and still,
> With measured motion, like a living thing
> Strode after me.
>
> —Wordsworth, *Prelude*, ll. 107–114

For many days after this terrifying experience his brain "Worked with a dim and undetermined sense/Of unknown modes of being" (ll. 121–122). His mind is full of "huge and mighty forms that do not live/Like living men" (ll. 127–128). These forms blot out the reassuring colours of everyday sights and trouble his dreams by night.

Wordsworth thought of this work as chronicling the ways in which his particular "strain of music" was built up, and he subtitled it "The Growth of a Poet's Mind". Readers from the helping professions will be interested in this eloquent exposition of a child's perception of self in relation to the bigger picture, in this case the power of nature. It also speaks to the child in the heart of the reader. Wordsworth himself lost both parents in childhood, and readers may see in it experiences of loss and abandonment similar to those, say, of contemporary looked-after children. We might say that this part of the *Prelude* documents a loss of innocence, but equally we might want to see it as an example of how experience is processed by an individual in a particular social context, and how the foundations of resilience are laid down. We could also note that Wordsworth was not only interested in "nature" but was also passionately concerned with social conditions and the politics of the age. The years in which Wordsworth began to write the *Prelude* were also those in which Europe was preoccupied with revolution and war and the "big picture" was one of social dislocation and political turmoil.

As a postscript on memoir we might want to look at a couple of books in which literary texts are used to anchor and to elaborate the personal story. Francis Spufford's book *The Child that Books Built* explores his own childhood through the books which absorbed him, body and mind, protecting him and giving him the means to come to terms with the difficulties of his young life. Also focused on the power of literature to aid endurance, *Reading Lolita in Tehran*, by Azar Nafisi, tells the story of a group of women who assembled on a weekly basis in Tehran during the late 1990s to read proscribed works of Western literature. The women's stories are contextualised by events in revolutionary Iran, the legacy of war and continuing civil unrest, and they are illuminated from within by their readings of such works as Jane Austen's *Pride and Prejudice*, F. Scott Fitzgerald's *The Great Gatsby*, Henry James's *Washington Square* and Nabokov's *Lolita*. The result is a mutually enriching blend of historical observation and literary reflection.

Novels

Novels composed of letters, diary entries and other documents are known by the term "epistolary". They occupy a position between journals and first person ("I") narratives and can create a semblance of "objective reality" through the presentation of multiple viewpoints, but readers have to beware of taking too much for granted. The writer may have deliberately introduced fallibility in documentation and narration, with the intention of unsettling the reader and undermining comfortable assumptions. This kind of writing is therefore most helpful reading for people wanting to practise a "not knowing" position! Epistolary novels became popular in the eighteenth century, in English with Richardson's *Pamela* and *Clarissa* and in French with Laclos's *Les Liaisons Dangereuses*. They fell out of fashion later in the century, and authors like Jane Austen went on to use an omniscient third person narrator instead. This kind of narrator is outside the story, looking on. There is no "I" voice, and the characters are referred to as "he", "she" and "they". This, of course, also positions the reader quite differently and quite firmly in the "knowledge and certainty" corner.

There is something intriguing about the epistolary form for writers and readers, however, especially when read with a more postmodern "lens". *The Color Purple*, by Alice Walker, is a good example of a story in which the power of language to construct personal identity is subverted by the inability of letters to communicate effectively in the absence of reliable writers and readers. Novels composed of different kinds of (fallible) document have also appealed to post-colonial writers, like Mariama Bâ's *Une Si Longue Lettre* ("So long a letter"—originally written in French in Senegal), Ruth Prawer Jhabvala's *Heat and Dust* (India) and Margaret Atwood's *The Handmaid's Tale* (Canada). Therapists accustomed to having to distinguish between the relative status of different kinds of communications and meanings simultaneously (verbal, non-verbal, contextual, etc.) may find it very interesting to track, at their leisure and outside the heat of the therapeutic moment, how this task is handled by writer and reader in one of these novels. In *We Need to Talk About Kevin*, by Lionel Shriver, the letter form consistently and effectively subverts the reader's expectations and understandings until the last page or two, whilst presenting a poignant, implied commentary on the mental state of the narrator, who is both partial in her story telling and fallible in her own grasp of the situation.

Several nineteenth century authors use the form, including Wilkie Collins in *The Moonstone* and *The Woman in White*. My favourite is Bram Stoker's *Dracula*, which combines spooky gothic horror with a fast-paced story of pursuit and detection. It is in fact a "rattling good yarn"! New (or indeed old) therapists may want to compare their position (especially if they are asked to make home visits) with that of the hapless Jonathan Harker, the recently qualified young lawyer sent to Transylvania to do business with the Count. He finds it remarkably difficult to exercise his professional judgment and protect himself appropriately in these circumstances. The Count demands that he write letters ready to send home anticipating the end of business. Jonathan smells a rat, and his diary entry states:

> "I would fain have rebelled, but felt that in the present state of things it would be madness to quarrel openly with the Count whilst I am so absolutely in his power; and to refuse would be to excite his suspicion and to arouse his anger … I saw in his eyes something of that gathering wrath which was manifest when he hurled that fair woman from him. He explained that posts were few and uncertain, and that my writing now would ensure ease of mind to my friends …" (Chapter 4, Jonathan Harker's Journal).

First person narratives are perhaps the most obvious resources for developing therapists, because in these texts personal reflections are set out most clearly, although the reader still has to look out for the odd fallible narrator. Because such narrators are usually also characters in the story, they are likely not to be party to some important pieces of information, like the anonymous "second Mrs de Winter" in Daphne du Maurier's *Rebecca*, or Nick Carraway in *The Great Gatsby*. Other narrators, like Benjy Compson in William Faulkner's *The Sound and the Fury*, tell only part of the story from a scrambled viewpoint. *The Curious Incident of the Dog in the Night-Time*, by Mark Haddon, presents "reality" through the eyes of an autistic narrator. This storyteller is not so much fallible as very different. He is actually a stickler for detail, much in the vein of his predecessor Sherlock Holmes, and the perspective he presents is challenging but refreshing. Novels like Anne Michaels's *Fugitive Pieces* are complex and multi-layered, reflecting the quality of human experience, especially during and after appalling trauma, and illustrating the shifting and uncertain nature of memory. This reminds me that one of the participants in my "literary reading and family therapy" study identified just this as an indispensable part of literary reading—that it never lets us forget that the mind builds up layer upon layer of meaning. We need not only to be aware that this is so, but also to learn to engage in an appropriately multi-layered way if we are to be truly helpful professionals.

Poetry

One of the great discoveries I have made in recent years is just how great poetry is as travel reading. It is usually contained in slim volumes and does not require that we master a mass of plot details in order to appreciate what is being said at any point, unless, that is, we are reading narrative poetry. Most can be picked up for ten minutes, then put down and picked up again for five, and it does not matter that you lose your place, because your place was only a temporary punctuation anyway. In other words its supreme portability makes it splendid company on public transport, in odd moments between clients, and when the mind wants a quick infusion of inspiration. Some poetry books can be read through like novels, as I did with Ted Hughes's *Birthday Letters* because it seemed to have a cumulative story to tell about a marriage. "The Lady of Shalott", who started this chapter, has a distinct story to tell and so is usually read through, although separate verses have huge impact on their own. Some poetry needs to be read in very small pieces because of its great emotional intensity, like Pascale Petit's *The Zoo Father*.

Poetry can express what is hard to say in other kinds of words. Another of the participants in my study said that she thought poetry represented our constant struggle with and for language. Therapists need to live and work more obviously in language than many other professionals, so poetry could (and arguably should) be as indispensable for us as scales for a pianist or warm-ups for an athlete. This is not to say that poetry is in a subordinate position to the other kinds of literature we have been discussing. Quite the reverse, in fact. We may "warm up" with poetry, but we may also choose poetry to match our most precious and profound moments.

Conclusion

This chapter has pulled out a few of the texts which are helpful reading for the journey of personal and professional development. We have looked in detail at some and have signposted many others.

This chapter aimed to say something about the craft of the therapist, which is to reach an integration of theory in practice. The theory we have to look at is very extensive, comprising not only what we need to exercise our particular therapeutic skills but also what we should know to be able to get alongside our clients in the part of their everyday lives which they are prepared to share with us. Family therapists started out with the theory of systems, including those of communication and control, and learned how they might be applied to family structures, sequences of behaviour, and beliefs. They then moved in the direction of biology and took theory from constructivists, and when that proved limited, replaced it with the language-based theory of social constructionism. We now seem to be at the point where there is some consensus that realities are generated in social intercourse between people, and this is the broad theoretical path we are going to follow.

But what about all the other knowledges we need, like: how does it feel to be a member of this group or that, or none? How do all our social and our spiritual motives and experiences relate to each other? What responsibilities do we have as professionals and as human beings to each other? How do we bring together the different kinds of mental processes and make meaning with them? These are the questions for our developmental journey, and this chapter has made some suggestions about what might help us on our way.

Exercise: Literary "maps"

CHAPTER FIVE

Enquiry: a valuable tool
for mountaineers

"Some change went through them all ... and they were all conscious
of making a party together in a hollow, on an island; had their common cause against that fluidity out there ... anything might happen,
she felt."

(Virginia Woolf, *To the Lighthouse*, 1927)

A scene

We are in a pleasant ground floor room at a popular northern
university. It is a September afternoon, several years ago. Pale
sunlight streams gently through the windows and student
voices drift in from the street. The room doubles as part of a
family therapy suite, but this afternoon its comfortable chairs
are occupied by seven new recruits (four women and three
men) for the Diploma/MSc in Systemic Psychotherapy. This is
the initial meeting of their Personal Development Group, and
I am trying to sell them the idea firstly of being my research
participants, and secondly of doing the whole thing with
literature. They are fresh and keen, though a little overwhelmed

by a dawning realisation of the huge commitment the course as a whole is demanding of them. They are intrigued by what I am proposing: that each of our meetings during the year should take as its format the sharing of literary extracts brought by each person. They also display a proper scepticism about being research participants at the same time as attending to their own personal development. They wonder what possible relevance the activity described might have to the training of a family therapist. It is difficult to keep myself on track and not retreat, then and there, from the whole idea. It seems simply too unusual and risky. We spend a good deal of time discussing the pros and cons. Eventually everyone agrees to give the idea a chance, and we embark on a voyage into the unknown.

I think I know where I want to go, based on ideas I have developed and a few workshops I have run. Of course none of us knows our destination. The route remains to be set by the literary voices and images group members decide to bring.

Literary reading and personal development

The trainees sitting together in the late September sunlight represented the most innovative part of a process of enquiry. The process had already taken me through a written survey method, the Delphi, and subsequent individual interviews of the participants. During the initial phases I had often wished the participants could talk to each other directly about such issues as: what would it mean for therapists to introduce literary material directly into work with clients? What does poetry demand from me as a reader? Just how much fascinating insight, into how many questions, can we get from this piece of writing? I knew already that the breadth and depth of appreciative conversation could be enhanced by the inclusion of multiple voices, so I wanted to supplement the individual perspectives with something more collective. I thought this would strengthen the research design, add interest, and broaden the scope of its relevance. Most exciting of all, however, was the prospect of trying out the notion that a literary focus could generate a unique learning environment which would be both stimulating and tailored precisely to the needs of the group itself. Literature was in the foreground from the outset, as I required participants to seek out something meaningful to them to bring along: a poem, a short extract from a novel, a song lyric. This, I thought, would promote a culture in which a more imaginative, intuitive, emotionally informed consciousness was seen to be the norm. Although some risk taking would be an essential part of participation, ultimately the environment would be safe and nurturing. A learning environment constructed in this way would complement the rest of the course and help develop therapeutic ability through experiential learning.

This view of personal/professional development (PPD) in training privileges personal experiences and feelings. It aims to foster a particular quality of being which is open and enabling, empathetic and creative. It involves learning to be alongside others in their most intimate and vulnerable life experiences, whilst retaining the ability to perceive and draw out possibilities not already present. This perspective is informed by ideas of social construction (the world of meaning generated through social intercourse in language), emphasising the co-construction of new realities between participants as the basis of therapeutic change. The "self" of the therapist is an essential tool in this approach. This perspective on PPD is a generic one, coherent with many therapeutic modalities and with training philosophies which recognise and value the particular combination of skills and knowledge required to practise the art of therapy.

The research journey

This chapter tells of the qualitative research effort which launched me on the "literature and therapy" expedition. I hope that readers who are not usually very interested in research will forgive a slight digression into qualitative methodology. During the enquiry, "texts" are produced by the recording of specifically focused talk. The analysis applied to these texts is not so very different from the critical approach we might make to literary poetry and prose.

The journey began with a survey method, the Delphi, which was devised in the 1970s (Linstone & Turoff, 1975) to take soundings and develop thinking among a group of knowledgeable people (Delphi panel) on a previously unexplored or contentious subject. In my study, the "panel" consisted of family therapists who were all senior clinical practitioners, teachers and writers. Participants wrote, in response to open questions, about the literary texts which had influenced them at different points in their lives. They also wrote about how they felt this reading had been, and still was, represented in their professional practice as clinicians, supervisors and teachers. The Delphi method is iterative (repetitive) and cumulative. It takes place in a number of "rounds" in which, after the first, the material from the previous round is pooled and re-presented for further comment. The first two rounds delineated the scope of the subject as already experienced by the participants. Further rounds could have been used to refine the opinions offered. As I was not really looking for refinement as much as new thinking, I decided to invite participants to individual interviews to explore their ideas in more depth and greater detail.

In the interviews, the participants and I talked *about* encounters with literature. Thematic analysis of the interviews revealed clusters of meaning and important concepts, like the all-important link between the language in which literature is framed (the language of literature) and the experiential world which is created by its reading (a different world). It also became clear that memories of reading, say in childhood, incorporate the circumstances of the reading as well as the story and text-based effects. The appearance of a book, its feel, and even its smell also carry meaning which is important to the reader. Elements of the reading experience, such as sitting with a parent or a child, taking refuge from, or trying to understand overwhelming life events, are evoked when revisiting the text.

The group was the third stage of the enquiry. It gave us the chance to *experience* literature-based discussion *directly and immediately*. The participants and I were now positioned *inside* the approach we were exploring. The talk produced by the group in active discussion was different from that generated by the interviewees—more provisional, spontaneous and freewheeling. It seemed less likely to be formed by the real or imagined expectations of the interviewer, and group members seemed to draw inspiration and confidence from each other. The nature of the resulting "text" demanded a different analytic and interpretive method from the one I had used for the individual interviews. The emphasis moved from an individual "phenomenological" viewpoint composed by the respondent for the formal requirements of an interview (albeit a semi-structured one) to a freer, dialogical, spur-of-the-moment, collective production. The group was encouraged by shared enthusiasm, and I felt bold enough to follow my instinct to investigate the way in which participants used and were used by strong currents of meaning or discourses. These came from all directions, struggling for expression in language.

This involved my looking at two levels: the surface, where expression is predominantly literal, and the figurative, which is concealed beneath the surface. In each group session a system of metaphors and figurative language evolved, drawn from the chosen literary extracts brought by the members. Participants were helped to reflect on painful personal dilemmas, using the language and images of the extracts. Each time we met, there was a point at which the group became completely immersed in the "literary" world, the process of collective meaning-making outstripping our ability and our desire to interpret. This produced an effect in which we seemed to be borne along on invisible streams of shared understanding.

Before this begins to sound too much like an episode of *The X Files*, let us rejoin the group, this time in our third session. The extract below illustrates one of these meaning "currents".

"Alps on Alps"

It is now March of the following year, and group members are all feeling the pressure. One person in particular is finding the going very tough, especially in balancing the demands of course/work/family. He feels extremely dispirited, and has brought with him the words of a moving song which expresses his feelings. He has imagined it being played at his funeral. There is a short, shocked pause. Then, tentatively, another group member comes in with the extract she has brought with her. It is by the eighteenth century poet Alexander Pope, and for the moment the link with the previous contribution remains inexplicit. It begins "A little learning is a dangerous thing" and continues after a few lines:

So pleased at first the tow'ring Alps we try,
Mount o'er the vales, and seem to tread the sky,
Th'eternal snows appear already past,
And the first clouds and mountains seem the last;
But, those attained, we tremble to survey
The growing labours of the lengthened way,

Th'increasing prospects tire our wand'ring eyes,
Hills peep o'er hills, and Alps on Alps arise!
—Alexander Pope, *An Essay on Criticism*, 1711

The atmosphere in the group room warms to the theme of mountaineering. Here is an extract of the discussion:

D: OK, so there's another mountain—and when I've finished this course there's going to be other mountains, but it's not that I've got to scale them all before I finish!
H: So it's about perspective. But there's also woods and snow and mountains.
T: There's the odd bit of plateau as well!
K: The reason you do climbing is usually to see the view.
D: And to look back. You know—I was there a while ago and now I'm here.
O: … or doing a route which is a bit risky, or you're unsure whether you can actually do it. That's when it's great—it's not as though you've parked at the car park and then got the cable car the rest of the way up.
H: You might get the same view at the top, but actually you haven't got the buzz inside you of achievement from conquering that challenge.
T: Oh yes you have! And you're not knackered—you can enjoy it!
H: No, you're never knackered at the top, you're knackered while you're doing it, but not at the top!
N: And if you're suffering in the name of a sport you love, like mountaineering, then it's a personal achievement. If you're dragged up there kicking and screaming, it's traumatic. If you're mountaineering and you clutch at a straw [reference to a previous theme], then you see that's not very good [laughter]. What you want is a bit of gear in the rock face, wearing a harness, and then someone else at the other end so that if you fall … I think what we need is a buddy system.
H: Funny you should mention that—there's actually a device you put in the rock that's called a "friend" and literally you use a "friend" to hold on tight, to anchor yourself safely to the rock.

In this short, rapid sequence the group moved from the brink of despair, feeling unable to offer mutual support, to a position which afforded glimpses of an optimistic future. The movement involved both hearts and minds. Hopelessness and weakness were transformed into the promise of strength and a vision of better things to come, and all without any explicit reference to the course or to themselves as trainees. The link between one person's distress and the transformative power of the mountaineering metaphor was intuitive, using the literary resource brought by one individual to gather and orchestrate the group response. The form of the poem, first on the page and then read aloud, gave the participants a rich medium for improvising on both internal and external personal states. If they wanted to, they could use the poet's words to express their own thoughts and feelings. The poet himself had already introduced an element of transformation: in this case by speaking of learning as an expedition through a mountainous landscape, where perspectives on achievement are constantly changing. The readers were drawn into this process and into a frame of mind which disposed them to wander among possibilities. Here they could find points of reference and pathways of elaboration which were emotionally and intellectually congruent.

Literary readers as researchers

Meanwhile I was busy with another kind of "reading" and transformation. The transcribed tapes of group sessions required careful analysis if we were to identify and recycle the benefits we had sampled. The session transcripts were treated as a single text. That is, I did not distinguish between the different voices represented. Figurative language constructs, like the complex of talk around the mountain and mountaineering metaphors above, were identified and their elaboration mapped. My reading of the transcripts suggested that figurative language operates in the "space between" people and also in the borders between the more and the less conscious parts of the mind. This contributes to an explanation of how a group of people can come together and find that they have been thinking about the same things (like T.S. Eliot's overcoat in Chapter Three), or along the same lines, even though they have not been conferring. They have elaborated their thinking under the influence of shared figurative constructs. These constructs can, and do, exert their influence below the threshold of conscious awareness. This, then, is an empirical manifestation of the theoretical ideas about image and metaphor advanced in Chapter Three.

In previous chapters we have considered literary reading and other literary practices in their relation to therapy, but there is also an argument for regarding qualitative enquiry as a practice involving reading and text-based discussion. Qualitative psychosocial research and therapy are both meaning-making exercises, and their relationship is ideally mutually informative. Therapy itself is a particular kind of enquiry. Systemic therapists have worked especially hard in the area of questioning (Palazzoli et al, 1980; Cecchin, 1987; Tomm, 1987, 1988) to fashion a method which, though usually involving some kind of strategy, is essentially open to the new and unexpected. Therapists are required by their training to be familiar with what already counts as knowledge, but they also have to be open in their work to new information. By the same token, researchers are now aware of the impact of their enquiry on the people and systems involved and how this affects what knowledge is acquired. Both have to be reflective and reflexive, and both are part of the landscape travelled through by the developing therapist. It makes a lot of sense, therefore, to consider them together, and the "reading" metaphor is good at highlighting their similarities.

The importance of image, metaphor and symbol in creating worlds of possibility is central in literary, therapeutic and, we may now think, research worlds. Energy and creativity, operating in the context of an empathic conversation about intimate and emotionally charged issues, are indicators of good therapy and healthy development. It is essential for therapists be aware of communication operating below the level of individuals' consciousness, and to recognise the conditions under which this kind of communication is facilitated. Our group members had just this kind of insight in the example above. Such moments may pass unnoticed in ordinary life, but the research process slows, focuses and records so that we can see the process in action.

Figurative language and the "different world" of literature

The image, reader response theorist Wolfgang Iser says, "is basic to ideation". Figurative language underpins the bridge between the reality of the everyday world and the intentional "irrealisation" of literature. Literature, as we noted previously, does not and cannot give a full and accurate account of everyday experience. It is inevitably full of holes, and this is what draws the reader into doing the imaginative work of literary reading. He suggests that the interrelationship of these different realities is what enables us to step outside the mundane "so that we can view our own world as a thing 'freshly understood'" (Iser, 1978, p. 140). In our group's conversation, a series of mental images, drawn from literary extracts like the song lyric and the words of Pope's poem, gave rise in turn to more and different images, like the vision of the fell walker bounding up the last bit of mountainous terrain to stand triumphantly at the top. They reflect various aspects of everyday reality and also give access to an imaginative world in which new possibilities are revealed and/or generated.

Stepping into the world of the imagination broadens the experiential horizon in all fields and forces us to think and feel beyond our customary limits. Amongst the devices which "recruit the reader's imagination", and enlist him in the "performance of meaning under the guidance of the text" (Bruner [quoting Iser], 1986, p. 25)—are metaphors. Bruner, rather appositely for our purposes, later describes these as "crutches to help us get up the abstract mountain" (1986, p. 48). The group participants found these "crutches" especially helpful when the going was tough.

Other ideas emerging from the study

The study, of which the group was part, began with a more individual focus. I asked some senior family therapists, supervisors and trainers to tell me about what they remembered reading through their lives, what kind of influence they felt this reading had had on their development, both personal and professional, and what use they were making of literary resources in their current work. Some familiar ideas first began to emerge at this time. Let's rewind a little to look at some of them in more detail.

Idea 1: A "reading history"

First and foremost there was confirmation of my hunch that participants would not only remember examples of influential reading from the past, but would also connect them with their personal/professional development to date. For several it was a surprisingly moving emotional experience. One of the interviewees said: "In a way this is more 'me' than anything else I've done." This insight led to the idea of the "reading history", a chronological review of influential reading across the lifespan, in which may be discerned developmental themes and patterns of attachment to particular stories, characters and forms of language. The term "attachment" seems appropriate because individuals' accounts of their literary experiences really did touch upon the growth of their sense of "other" and, in turn, their sense of "self". An exercise making use of this idea is at the foot of the present chapter. The vignette below explores the idea.

Vignette: "How **did** things get to be the way they are?"

Virginia, a woman of 35, is seeking help with the persistent sense of pointlessness which is spoiling her life. She no longer enjoys her job as a PE teacher, and feels at a loss to know how to improve her social life. This has taken a nose dive since splitting up with her male partner some three months before. She is unwilling to participate in conversations which define her problems as anything to do with her own mental health, relationships with family members, or the past in general.

The therapist respectfully suggests that without some looking back to the past it will be very difficult to understand the present, let alone do something about it. How would it be to explore a developmental trajectory in a slightly different way? Maybe by tracing some of the things she has been excited by during her life? Does she like reading, for example?

As it happens, Virginia's second subject is English, and although she cannot see the point yet, she is prepared to discuss her "reading history". Little by little she gains confidence in talking about her relationships with literary texts as varied as Enid Blyton's *Famous Five* and George Eliot's *The Mill on the Floss*. She now only reads the newspaper and educational journals. Her greatest surprise is to remember how much she loved the writings of Simone de Beauvoir, which she read at school as part of her French course. She recalls in some detail how these writings spoke to her personally and how engaged she felt, not only with the ideas but also with the texts themselves. She and the therapist begin to trace several themes, amongst which (drawing on the writings which so inspired her as a girl) is that of gender identity and how questions of sexuality and sexual orientation can be opened up in positive and creative ways.

Whilst still having no definitive answers to her predicament, Virginia resolves to join a women's reading group. She feels she has found a different perspective on some of her personal tensions and has gained in confidence and energy from revisiting, through her favourite reading of the time, a period of her life which was more optimistic and less fixed.

A couple of years later the therapist hears that Virginia has returned to university and is completing a Masters degree in Women's Writing. She is living on her own and enjoying it.

Idea 2: Externalising and commonality

Second is the notion that literature (broadly interpreted) provides an external focus which can bring people together in addressing painful or dangerous-feeling topics. In some ways it can also help to "level the playing field" between therapist and client. This is because literature is a resource which is essentially in the public domain, belongs to no-one, and is susceptible to multiple interpretations. There is, of course, the question of literacy and access to reading materials, but this problem disappears if the definition of literature is sufficiently wide. Almost everyone has a favourite song, image or story. Study participants were divided on the question of whether or not a therapist should suggest something to read to a client. Some were reluctant, even though they felt that literary reading had been beneficial for their own development, because they felt there was a danger that it would be an unwarranted intrusion and imposition on vulnerable clients. Others said: "It helped me, so why wouldn't I want to share it with this child or this family?" Another aspect of this is that the characteristic external focus provided by the use of literary resources can help a disorganised and mutually unsupportive group to achieve coherence. The following vignette explores a use of this idea in a community network context.

Vignette: "We just don't know how to talk about this!"

A few years ago a secondary school suffered a tragic sequence of disasters. A series of accidents meant that five pupils died in various incidents over just a few weeks. The young people's own families struggled to continue with their lives in the face of such horrors. The school did all the things a good school should try to do, but a year later some members of staff were finding it hard to come to terms with what had happened. It wasn't that they had been neglected, or that their burden was heavier than expected under the circumstances. It was just that somehow they hadn't been able to talk together and support each other in the way they needed.

A regular lunchtime get-together for local professionals at the local CAMHS Clinic is often well attended by school staff who have particular professional interests in pastoral care. It is a place to eat your lunch, do some networking, and talk together about topics of interest within a loose frame of systemic thinking. When staff from the school in question asked if they could suggest "bereavement" as a topic and possibly raise some of their own collective issues for consultation, the facilitators had to think hard about how to introduce the topic of adult responses to child death. They felt confident that there was a need which had not so far been met and wanted to create a facilitative environment which would allow individuals to voice personal thoughts and feelings (a risk in itself) in as safe and constructive a way as possible. They were wary, at the same time, of overwhelming the short lunchtime meeting. It seemed that, so far, conditions had been missing to enable individuals to give voice to what might be experienced as negative, or even possibly hurtful or offensive, by others. It was important to be mindful of the needs of other group participants, without falling into the trap of prematurely closing down any risky-sounding themes, thereby perpetuating the unsatisfactory status quo.

The facilitators chose to start the meeting with a short extract from Stephen King's novella "The Body". The extract is a kind of meditation on the body of a boy killed in an accident on the railway line. They thought it moving, and sufficiently realistic to give "permission" for the expression of personal reflections of all sorts. It captured the horror of untimely deaths and also highlighted the way in which the imagination can run traumatic pictures on a kind of loop which continues to play long after the event is over. The facilitators hoped that others would be emboldened to reflect in a helpful way. They had to trust the natural externalising quality of literature, combined with their own group leadership skills, for this.

In the event the group didn't dwell on the text for long, but the atmosphere it created seemed very enabling. See what you think of this little snippet. In the story, four boys have set out to find the body of a contemporary who, they hear, has been accidentally killed on the railway line some miles from town. The narrator, who later becomes a well-known writer and speaks here in his older voice, relates the finding of an empty pair of shoes beside the railway track. In this excerpt, the truth of what he is looking at begins to dawn:

> For a moment I was puzzled—why was he here and the tennies [tennis shoes] there … Then I realised, and the realisation was like a dirty punch below the belt. My wife, my kids, my friends—they all think that having an imagination like mine must be quite nice; aside from making all this dough, I can have a little mind-movie whenever things get dull. Mostly they're right. But every now and then it turns around and bites the shit out of you with those long teeth, teeth that have been filed to points like the teeth of a cannibal. You see things you'd just as soon not see, things that keep you awake until first light. I saw one of those things now, saw it with absolute clarity and certainty. He had been knocked spang out of his Keds [trainers].The train had knocked him out of his Keds just as it had knocked the life out of his body.
>
> That finally rammed it all the way home for me. The kid was dead. The kid wasn't sick, the kid wasn't sleeping. The kid wasn't going to get up in the morning any more or get the runs from eating too many apples or catch poison ivy or wear out the eraser on the end of his

Ticonderoga No. 2 during a hard math test. The kid was
dead; stone dead. [King, 1982]

By the way, "The Body" is available in a special simplified text as a
Penguin Reader.

Idea 3: "Different possibilities in the world of literature?"

Third was the recognition that the world of literature is different
in kind from that of everyday life, and that a certain amount of
effort is required to pass into it. In other words it needs dedicated
time, a degree of practice, and a conviction that it will not be time
and effort wasted. This is important because the world of literature
offers possibilities which may be lost when we use language only
to convey information about something else. It is the literary use of
language, language creating something which we appreciate for its
own sake, which opens the door. Therapists need to know this kind
of world, inhabit it from time to time, and learn to use its resources.
The "different worldliness" of the literary is in part ascribable to its
metaphorical nature and the characteristic use of figurative language
and invocation of mental images. The comment below explores the
conditions which help to promote openness to this difference.

Comment on Idea 3: "It's a whole different world!"

Earlier in the chapter, we left our group of trainees sharing the pains
and pleasures of a clinical training through the medium of a literary metaphor. They were a resourceful cohort and went on beyond
the dedicated research time to share their continuing development
in similar ways until the end of their course. They had not been
pre-selected in any way, and certainly not for their abilities, or even
interest, in literary reading. Other groups in other places have had
very similar encounters, so I'd like to return to them for a moment,
just to consider the ways in which a context was created to enable
them to enter the world of "the literary" and to have the opportunity to experience at first hand the enabling propensities of literary
metaphor.

The group had a dual dedication: to the trainees' personal/pro-
fessional development and also to enquiring into the usefulness

of focusing on literature as a means of facilitating such a group. It was therefore a good example of cross-fertilisation between an experiential learning process and qualitative research. As noted above, interviewees in the study expressed strong opinions about the difficulty of entering the literary world. This is especially so when the mind is preoccupied with "getting the facts", "focusing", going straight to the "bottom line" and avoiding ambiguities and uncertainties, all of which figure prominently in, say, achieving targets, workload management, and so on. I was recently at a Medical Humanities Conference, which was attended by a mixture of medical practitioners and other helping professionals, alongside writers and artists. There I heard a young artist say that arts and health practitioners would never manage to converge if they (the health practitioners) continued to be obsessed with "summarising", "clarifying", "focusing", and making bulleted PowerPoint presentations of everything. The arts are not about these things; they are rather the antithesis, being generally more concerned with "opening up", improvising and making intuitive connections. The artist was restating the impossibility of approaching the arts via ways of thinking and acting which are more related to positivistic scientific methods. Experience persuades me that both kinds of approach need to develop side by side to achieve a healthy balance. To achieve this, therapists may have to learn to respect the "evidence" of their own feelings and intuitions.

The PPD group needed a protected space and dedicated time for this task. Creating a fertile context was important, and the first step was to take care in establishing the session format—each person to bring an extract which had "spoken" to them recently about the topic in question, i.e. their personal/professional development. In other groups, participants sometimes wanted to bring things like objects with inscriptions, and since I could not "know better" than the person in question, they did so, always with interesting results. Facilitators in such groups may have to take extra care to adhere to "fair shares" of time for all, even if some participants are keen to fade into the background. All extracts (or sometimes memories of stories or extracts) are worthy of being treated seriously, and enough time should be given to develop appropriate reflections.

In this case a body of theory was being developed about using literature in PPD and in clinical work. I shared as much of my experience of using literature as I could. As part of the research process, proceedings of the group were recorded and transcribed, the resulting texts shared with the participants, and feedback given and received. The devil's advocate would probably ascribe the positive benefits to a "Hawthorne effect", where the performance of participants in a study was enhanced for no other reason than that they simply participated and were being studied. There may be an element of this supplied by the intense scrutiny of the research process. However, since the effects were, and are, similar in many other groups and situations, it seems that the introduction of a literary focus brings its own rewards. These are: safe but stimulating sharing of otherwise difficult material; enrichment of discourse through inclusion of literary voices; operation of communication levels, both on and below the surface.

Conclusion

In this chapter we have visited a qualitative research study of therapists' literary reading. We have met a couple of groups and some individuals who used literature to pursue important personal and contextual issues for themselves. Ideas emerging from the study, like the "reading history", have particular relevance for individuals who would like to rewind aspects of their lives, or revisit the formative influences in their personal development. We have also visited the notion that literary reading in particular, and the arts in general, both generate and depend upon a "different world" of consciousness and association. The PPD group experience demonstrated that the use of a literary focus could help people communicate easily, and with depth and richness, about painful or contentious topics.

The quote which heads up the chapter is part of Virginia Woolf's description of the house party in her beautiful, funny, reflective novel *To the Lighthouse*. Guests and family are seen through the eyes of Mrs Ramsay as she surveys the coming together of husband, children and friends to eat dinner. Just for a moment she sees them bound together with a particular coherence and purpose, which is created by the candlelight of the table and the blackness of the surrounding night. A subtle change runs through them. A similar transformation occurs with the trainee group as they share their verses and images.

Families and groups, however, are all unique, along with the imaginative constructions we make around them. Virginia Woolf's magical vision is one thing. Stella Gibbons's grim collection of the denizens of Cold Comfort Farm is quite another, as they gather at the behest of Aunt Ada Doom, who, it may be recalled, "saw something nasty in the woodshed" and was never the same again. There "have always been Starkadders at Cold Comfort", and tonight (in the following extract) they have to be counted—just to make sure that nothing ever changes!

> The great kitchen was full of people. They were all silent, and all painted over by the leaping firelight with a hellish red glow. Flora could distinguish Amos, Judith, Meriam, the hired girl; Adam, Ezra, and Harkaway; Caraway, Luke, and Mark, and several of the farm hands. They were all grouped, in a rough semicircle, about someone who sat in a great high backed chair by the fire. The dim gold lamplight and the restless firelight made Rembrandt shadows in the remoter corners of the kitchen, and threw the dwarf and giant shadows of the Starkadders across the ceiling.
>
> ...
>
> Everybody was staring at the door. The silence was terrific. It seemed the air must burst with its pressure, and the flickering movement of the light and the fireglow upon the faces of the Starkadders was so restlessly volatile that it emphasised the strange stillness of their bodies. Flora was trying to decide just what the kitchen looked like, and came to the conclusion that it was the Chamber of Horrors at Madame Tussaud's. [Gibbons, 1932]

In the end, be it Ramsays or Starkadders, the principle is the same. Get together with some candlelight or a nice fire, in a good book, and anything might happen!

Exercise: Sharing the load

CHAPTER SIX

Reading and writing

"Writers have to start out as readers ..."
(Seamus Heaney, *The Redress of Poetry*, 1995)

"My writing is simply a set of experiments in life—an endeavour to see what our thought and emotion may be capable of."
(George Eliot, letter 25 January 1876)

"Writing is very improvisational. It's like trying to fix a broken sewing machine with safety pins and rubber bands. A lot of tinkering."
(Margaret Atwood, *Conversations*, 1990)

This chapter brings our journey to a stopover point to consider the relationship between two literary practices: reading and writing. These two activities complement each other as they stand in creative tension. There is no reading without writing, and it could be argued that writing only becomes meaningful when it is read. They are interdependent activities. In the early 21st century, writing exists in a multitude of forms and serves many purposes. Three short scenes give a sense of the scope of our topic.

Vignette 1

A group of ten FT trainees are at their respective homes one weekend, going about their usual business. Some are engaged in routine domestic or recreational tasks and, because all are busy helping professionals, some are catching up with a bit of relaxation. At some point in the day they each check their emails and find a message from their trainers who, because teaching time is short, are trying out some distance learning and tutorial methods.

They are asked to suggest some hypotheses or "educated guesses" about what systemic (contextual, relational) patterns can be discerned in an attached case study, and to offer their implications for future professional intervention. Responses are to be written according to a specific prescription known as a "formulation" and returned to the trainers, who will contribute their thoughts. All the writing will be visible to all the trainees and their tutors. This process is intended to aid the trainees' skill development, to generate new ideas and to stimulate discussion. Formulations can be used to structure and inform treatment plans, and are the basis of spoken and written exchanges between professional and family and/or individual, and between professionals.

Several are uncertain about whether to bother with this extra, non-assessable piece of work intruding unbidden into their private space. Others, however, are hooked by the email form and the way it eases the transition between familiar, everyday note jotting and the specialist writing and reading habits they are trying to acquire—and not only writing but talking and listening too.

Vignette 2

Another group, this time a mixture of helping professionals at a conference, sit in a silent and thoughtful circle, nibbling or gently tapping the ends of their pens and pencils. After a few minutes, first one begins to write, and then another, and another, until they are all scribbling energetically. They have all chosen to attend a "writing workshop" to sample the benefits of reflective writing, with the idea of enhancing their personal and professional development. They might even decide to incorporate it directly in their work.

This writing feels like a very private practice. That feeling changes when the workshop leader asks for a volunteer to read and, slowly at first, one after another, each person surrenders their contribution to the group. The experience is at once stimulating and daunting. Some participants are old hands, whilst for others this is their first writing workshop and, they determine, their last.

Most people will remember what they wrote and how they felt in this workshop for years to come.

Vignette 3

Two family therapists are discovered alone in a large room furnished with easy chairs. The setting is a community mental health service for children, adolescents and their families. A large and thought-provoking mural of the Simpsons gazes down at them from one wall. The blind has been pulled down over the one-way screen and the client family have departed. The pair sprawl in their comfy chairs, looking a bit despondent. The session did not move forward in quite the way they hoped, and so much was left unsaid and unheard on both sides. Did they, the therapists, really convey the admiration they felt for the family's courage in the face of terrible adversity? They had tried hard to give voice to a more positive view of the situation, not only because they were convinced it created a more realistic balance, but because they saw it as a way to bring clients and therapists together in a common task.

Both clinicians fear that the family members were so overwhelmed with the demands of their daily lives and the effort of bringing themselves to the session that they may not have heard, or accepted, the therapists' reflections. Now the family have left, there seems to be little basis for further discussion.

This is a depressing prospect for the therapists, who are well aware of the connotations of powerlessness attached to seeking help from an agency such as theirs. They wanted very much to connect with family members and, in so doing, to highlight their strengths as well as their fragility. In this way they hoped that the family's interpersonal problems could be transcended for a vital moment. Unless family members can feel more able to use their own considerable resources, they are likely to remain bogged down in conflict over relatively trivial matters.

The therapists decide to write a letter.

Reading and writing

Previous chapters have focused on reading as a literary practice. This chapter considers writing: the kind we can do for ourselves. This book has so far featured writing which is published, to which people ascribe the title "literature", and which ranges from the poetry of Shakespeare to the novels of Stephen King. We are now introducing a different kind of text and a variation in the relationship between text and writer/reader. It may be a good time, therefore, to revisit the focus on our area of interest, which is the contribution, actual and potential, which literary practices can make to therapists' own development, their clinical practice, and thereby to their clients. Readers of this chapter will inevitably feel that we have merely passed over the surface of a vast, deep pool. The aim here, however, is not comprehensiveness. There are many excellent books entirely devoted to the subject, including reflective, therapeutic and personal development writing. This chapter presents some theory and practice perspectives which fit with the overall theme of this book, which is the "different world" which takes shape when we participate in literary practices like reading, writing and improvising conversations around texts which have been composed with meaning-making in mind.

Everyday writing ranges from a few notes we make to record a clinical session, to something which is carefully constructed to give form to thoughts and/or feelings which may not be readily expressed otherwise. We have seen that reading is a dialogical process involving writer, reader and text. In reading, there is a continuous interaction between reader and text, and meaning is generated in the space between them. It is not, of course, that the words on the page change. Literary texts are constructed in such a way as to facilitate or create space for multiple interpretations, and to provoke elaboration and improvisation in the mind of the reader. Writing, however, really does begin with a blank page and the prospect of a text that is infinitely variable. Or at least that's how it seems.

In her paper "Our 'Other History': Poetry as Meta-Metaphor for Narrative Therapy" (1996), Maryhelen Snyder proposes that we can extend and enrich the familiar idea of "authoring" if we proceed beyond the "story" metaphor and adopt a "poetry" metaphor. This would mean that we see people not only as storytellers to self and others in their own lives, but as poets too. This would enable us to encompass "that which cannot be reduced to any story". She elaborates this notion with reference to an idea of "aesthetic knowing" or "poetic intelligence", of which more will be said below. In this paper she includes a short extract from *Harland's Half Acre*, a novel by Australian novelist David Malouf (1984), which precisely suits the stage we have reached in thinking about writing in the context of therapeutic practice. This quotation is about an artist contemplating the blank whiteness of a sheet of paper. Malouf is describing the act of drawing, but it works equally well for writing: "The page was his mind and contained everything that was in his mind and which waited there to be brought forth. Hidden beneath it was the world. He had only to let things emerge, to let his hand free them."

With this view of the author and blank sheet in mind, we might say that there are particular people in the picture, or on the page, with their own quirks and nuances, right from the outset. Any kind of writing must arise initially from what is already in the mind of the writer, even if this is just a space where ideas, feelings or intuitions might grow. This is not all, however. Reader response theorist Wolfgang Iser suggests that every text is written with an implied reader in mind. This reader "embodies all those predispositions necessary for a literary work to exercise its effect—predispositions laid down not by an empirical outside reality but by the text itself" (1978, p. 34). Iser is talking about literary text and how it shapes the notional reader. It could also be argued that every piece of text, from a shopping list to an intensely personal poem, is written with a particular audience in mind, even if this is supposed to be the author alone. Celia Hunt, a writing teacher and researcher, noted that some creative writing students seemed inhibited in their writing of fictionalised autobiography because of the judgments they felt might be made. There was "a sense of readership or audience in the mind of a writer" during the writing process. This "implicit reader", who is present throughout the writing process, affects "what is written and the way writers represent themselves through their writing" (Hunt, 2004).

Sometimes we can be pretty sure that ostensibly private writing is actually framed to have a particular impact on a specific reader or readers. This may or may not become an overt strategy, and intended recipients may never be aware that messages are being sent their way. The poetry and songs which express the pain and disaffection of anguished youth more often than not remain generic and un-received by their intended readers. The "implicit reader" is the only one. Sometimes, however, "private" writing may be more clearly an indirect communication: the adolescent, for example, who leaves a secret diary where it is certain to be found by an anxious parent, or the email which is left on an accessible computer.

Vignettes

Let's look at the vignettes above. The range of situations included here reflects, in a small way, the breadth of writing possibilities in the early 21st century. **Vignette 1** highlights the ubiquity of writing/reading now we have the internet and email. Writing opportunities actually come looking for you in the privacy of your own home, and if you don't take them you are likely to be left behind. Emailing blurs the boundary between talking and writing. It is a seductive medium, creeping into our lives under a cloak of convenience and accessibility, but it can also be an insidious thief of time and a fertile growing medium for misunderstandings and misreading of the social signals which are usually straightforward in face-to-face talk. Its place in our lives is undeniable, and in any case the genie is out of the bottle. *Writing Cures* (Bolton et al, 2004) has no fewer than five chapters concerned with therapeutic writing online, but the context it provides is rather different from more traditional creative or academic settings.

Electronic communication is everywhere, and in many everyday instances has replaced other kinds of writing. I don't rush to look in my post box any more, for example, because most significant correspondence comes through my broadband connection. Many business and social agencies have already insisted that all internal and most external communication be made in this form.

Contemporary lifestyles are constructed increasingly around the constant availability of information and instant communication, to the extent that it begins to feel risky to venture out without a mobile phone or start the day without switching on the computer. So where do we find the space traditionally thought necessary for reflective writing, and why is it important?

In a study of the therapeutic benefits of autobiographical writing for creative writing students, a group of such students were prompted to engage in a guided fantasy to identify their ideal writing environment. They described "remote locations ... where the natural world is abundantly present". Participants wanted clarity of light and a sense of relationship between exterior and interior features. Celia Hunt (the researcher) invokes, by way of explanation, the Winnicottian idea of a "transitional realm", a "potential space" which "partakes of both psychic reality and the outside world" (Hunt, 2004). This is the sort of space which could also be described as a "liminal" or "in between" state characterised by indeterminacy and openness. "Liminality" is a description which comes from the Latin word for a threshold, and has been used in anthropology to describe stages in a ritual ("preliminary" and "subliminal" are related descriptions) and by social scientists to denote a marginal space which is uniquely valuable for the generation of meaning. This is the kind of environment that Hunt's students were imagining and hankering after to facilitate their self-exploration.

Creative space is also important in therapy. Arguably, most relational growth takes place in the borderlands between people and their worlds. In their seminal paper "Creating a Participant Text: Writing, Multiple Voices, Narrative Multiplicity", Penn and Frankfurt (1994) propose that introducing writing into therapy enables the writer to discover or invent other "voices" which can dialogue amongst themselves in the "space between", counteracting the effects of an existing "negative monologue". The exchange thus created can change our conversations with others because "in the act of writing, meanings that have been ignored or have remained unsaid are invited into the relational field by way of the text" (Penn & Frankfurt, 1994). This is a clear benefit for therapy. Undoubtedly there is a debate to be had about the place of email in this precious indeterminate area, and since it is impossible to put the electronic genie back in its bottle, its use in everyday writing repertoires is bound to persist and develop. The students in the vignette can choose between seeing this as a useful extension of their learning environment; an intrusion into their private space; an invitation to creativity; a combination of all three; or something completely different.

Vignette 2 takes us back to the type of writing which is branded "reflective" and may be part of an overall approach to practice for helping professionals (Bolton, 2005; Bolton et al, 2004). Reflective writing is a uniquely valuable medium for the promotion of reflexive, or self-conscious (in the best possible way!) self development. This is the kind of writing which we would hope to find in learning logs/reflexive journals created by people actively seeking to develop their own personal and professional abilities. Writing workshops in general may offer a range of benefits, from supportive encouragement for the self-esteem, confidence and empowerment of members to profound imaginative and spiritual experience such as that described by James Hillman as "soul making" (Hartill, 1998). A writing workshop is one way of exploring this activity and of comparing the practices and requirements of different professional groups.

The need for a creative space is highlighted in reflective writing exercises. This space is really a state of mind, and while it may be described in visual terms, it is also implied by some more abstract ideas like the "aesthetic knowing" or "poetic intelligence" described by Snyder. Peggy Penn, herself a poet, enlarged on the idea of "aesthetic knowledge" in an article she contributed to *Context* (news magazine of the Association for Family Therapy) in 2004. She reminds us that Plato defined aesthetics as "the pursuit of the good, the true, the beautiful". A space for writing, or other creative activity, is more than a state of mind. It is also a bodily phenomenon where aesthetic experience is valued. It exists in "the recognition of the breaking of pattern or the recognition of a pattern fit, a state of ecstasy, experiencing the flow, the whole, a synthesis, a powerful expressive state or a passionate curiosity. It can be understood as a new perspectival stance, sometimes occurring when moving away from origins and old definitions or when acquiring new insights" (Penn, 2004, p. 31). A writing workshop aims to enable participants to experience at least some of this "knowledge", so that they can take it back into their usual existence and use it to refresh practice and enliven day-to-day writing and talking.

Vignette 3 reminds us that therapy can be supplemented by extensions of therapeutic discourse through, say, the writing of letters (White & Epston, 1990). Therapists may write to clients, and patients/clients may offer expressive and exploratory writing to therapists (Ryle, 2004). These and other kinds of writing, as part of therapy, have gained considerable importance in the past couple of decades, both in therapeutic work which is labelled "narrative" and in other approaches. Collaborative writing is writing "with" clients rather than "to" or "about" them, and is designed to encourage participation in therapy (Bacigalupe, 1996). This could include exchanging notes of what happened in a session. Clients may bring notes of events which occur between sessions, and what my colleagues and I call "good days diaries," in which children and their families record, with whatever pictures, decorations and embellishments they wish, occasions on which things have gone OK. Very often such a diary contains pictures, and sometimes it includes poems and stories. Even when the text is virtual (e.g. "we thought about it a lot but not much got written down"), the idea of arranging language in a particular form to encompass a new way of describing an old situation usually enables participants to reposition themselves (e.g. "we didn't get round to writing it down but we can talk about how we see things now").

In their book *Narrative Means to Therapeutic Ends*, White and Epston highlight the differences between spoken and written language, concluding that "in our culture, recourse to the written tradition in therapy promotes the formalisation, legitimation, and continuity of local popular knowledges, the independent authority of persons, and the creation of a context for the emergence of new discoveries and possibilities." They also identify the contribution that writing can make in therapy "insofar as it facilitates the mapping of experience onto the temporal dimension" (1990, p. 34–35). In other words, writing pinpoints a moment in time, capturing growth and the development of meaning.

The letter which these therapists write will be, in essence, an extension of the session talk. It will be offered in the spirit of a conversational interchange. It is not an opportunity for the therapists to have the last word, but enables all participants to have something on paper to contemplate and reflect on in their own time. It will also mark a particular point in the lives of the participants. It is partly conceived out of the therapists' conviction that there is more to be said, and heard, than the confines of the session allowed. The therapists do not want so much to have their say as to loosen the boundaries of the conversational space. They want to make space for the view that the family has strengths and resources which can be mobilised in the service of resilience, creativity and health. This is almost certainly at variance with the predominant way these family members see themselves, both individually and as a group. The therapists will invite a written or telephone response in the hope of prolonging the discussion and presenting a possible "minority view". Their actions are based on a complex of theories and experience, but if asked, they might say that their main motivation is a kind of discomfort they feel at the shape of the conversation which has just finished. It "feels" incomplete and sits uncomfortably in the context created by the combination of family/therapy agency and all their surrounding networks. We might call this their ecology, following the terminology of Bateson (1972) and Keeney (1983).

On an ordinary day, the therapists will complete their work, pack up and go home without giving much thought to whether their work owes more to their competence as craftspeople or as artists. If pressed to analyse their intuition, however, they might think to pick up a well-thumbed volume, possibly falling apart at the spine like mine, in which Gregory Bateson writes of the importance of attending to the recursive relationship between different levels of mental process. An aesthetic response, he says, is a response to the "pattern which connects" (1979). It might surprise and please them to be reminded that their intuitive sense of the session's incompleteness is "aesthetic". Letter writing enacts an impulse which is primarily artistic and governed by the need to respond to their work in its ecological context. Thinking about writing helps to slow down the process and reveal the nature of accepted therapeutic practices which might otherwise be hidden. The writing itself is a performance of the kind of "aesthetic knowing" which we have already discussed—an attempt to "generate multiple descriptions", following Penn's exhortation to "Start with no maps, just create a space in where conversation can happen and, by itself, it will generate language and possibilities" (2004).

Why write in therapy and health care?

A good deal of work has been done in evaluating the usefulness and healing potential of literary practices—reading and writing, but mostly writing—in the more general field of health psychology (Lowe, 2004; Smyth et al, 1999) and occupational and public health (Philipp, 1996, 1997, 1999; Philipp et al, 1996). These initiatives are related to work by biomedical researchers (Pennebaker, 1997; Pennebaker et al, 1988) which showed some gains in immune response over time for a group of college student subjects who had written about personal traumatic experiences. Writing, they showed, is good for you, and although the reasons why may not be so clear, findings do suggest that the uses of literary (and other) arts may have a good psycho-biological basis (Lowe, 2000). Jeannie Wright has made a review of the literature in therapeutic writing, concluding, with Esterling et al, (1999, p. 94), that for many people "writing itself is a powerful therapeutic technique" (Wright, 2004). Writing is not universally beneficial, however, and the initial impact of writing about traumatic experiences may be overwhelming for unsupported writers, including maybe some engaging in therapy "online". More examples are discussed by Gillie Bolton in her book *Reflective Practice* (2005, pp. 62–63), especially in relation to the reduction of anxiety and stress and the pursuit of personal development.

Researchers and clinicians continue to be interested in the relationship between writing and health, and the literature flourishes. A "Reference list of writing/disclosure studies" compiled at the University of Texas contains at least 150 published papers and books from medical, psychological and other social science publications in English across the world. *Writing Cures* (Bolton et al, 2004) features in this list and contains a useful chapter reviewing the literature (Wright, 2004).

Practitioners who want to use writing in their routine work are likely to be most interested in when, how and why writing promotes health and aids the therapeutic process. Fiona Sampson, who has much experience as writer in residence in a variety of health care settings, says that the introduction of writing in mental health care settings "can allow clients to assume the authoritative position of the narrator and explore what they can formulate in language (symbol) and how." A key feature of this exploration is the acquisition of skills in writing. Whereas many of the studies of writing may focus on "expressive" writing and emotional disclosure in writing, Sampson emphasises the importance of engaging in the struggle for expression through learning the craft of writing. For example, she mentions "technically sophisticated poetry" which, alongside reading and writing to explore the writer's experiences, can help people reposition themselves with more consciousness of their subjectivity and more narrative control (Sampson, 1997). Joe Bidder, co-founder of Survivors' Poetry, echoed this point in an interview on BBC Radio 4's "All in the Mind" (25 April 2006, available at www.bbc.co.uk). He reiterates that it is not just expression of emotional and personal experience which is important but the processing of this experience through the discipline of writing which is also shared with a group of peers. Empirical evidence suggests that "many people, perhaps most, are able to guide their own therapy. Writing itself is a powerful therapeutic technique" (Esterling et al, 1999, p. 94). We have to remember that development of technique is an essential accompaniment of emotional expression if writing is to achieve its full potential.

Re-authoring lives: narrative and therapy

Readers, especially those coming from a systemic family therapy background, will be familiar with the importance of narrative approaches and methods in the field of psychotherapy, and the special developmental relationship which has existed between family and narrative therapies (http://www.dulwichcentre.com.au/questions.html). Narrative ideas are now very influential in therapeutic discourse, in the thinking of the helping professions and in the studies labelled "Humanities". The idea that we live "storied" lives now just seems like common sense. Where there are narratives, there are authors and audiences—hence their inclusion here. In earlier chapters we touched on the narrative metaphor and the way it shapes therapy, by proposing that therapeutic change involves re-authoring, and the re-discovery and re-instatement of preferable lived stories. We looked, too, at the claims for a more "poetic" or broadly aesthetic metaphor, which emphasises the way in which narratives are framed, drawing therapeutic participants into regard for the form as well as the content of their interchanges. Writing a predicament into a poem, for example, is likely to transform its meaning in ways which go beyond simple discussion and recording.

As well as the general notion of "authorship" in lived experience, narrative approaches include writing as part of a therapeutic process. White and Epston (1990), as noted above, explore the uses of writing in therapy and give examples of letters for a variety of purposes including invitation (as a tool of engagement), redundancy (to mark the passage of a redundant role), and so on, all as part of a storied therapy. They also discuss the substitution of letters for case records, and the differences in the meanings which can be generated in this way for all participants and possible audiences. Letters, they say, are "a version of that co-constructed reality called therapy and become the shared property of all parties to it" (White & Epston, 1990, p. 126).

Writing in search of self

In earlier chapters we have thought about reading literature as a life-long search for, and elaboration of, our sense of ourselves. We are, if we choose, in a continuous circular or reciprocal relationship with what we read. The writer is in a similar "dance" with what is written. This is most obvious, in literary terms, where novels, poems and songs are declaredly autobiographical, like John Clare's "I am", or—a century later—some poems of Anne Sexton and Sylvia Plath. *The Bell Jar*, Plath's fictionalised autobiography, reveals a view of her own troubled life in its social context. Virginia Woolf's *To the Lighthouse* is another example. Woolf herself was very interested in how subjective mental states could be conveyed in language. She also seems to have been fascinated by self in relation to context, not only the surrounding objects and landscape but also social networks both intimate and public. *To the Lighthouse* is about a family and friends at a seaside house party. In it, Woolf experiments with conveying not only interior personal states but shared "intersubjective" experience. The writing of this novel was also an important developmental task, especially focusing on her relationship with her parents. In her diary for 1928 she says: "I used to think of him and mother daily; but writing The Lighthouse laid them in my mind"; and much later, in "A Sketch of the Past": "I wrote the book [*To the Lighthouse*] very quickly; and when it was written, I ceased to be obsessed by my mother. I no longer hear her voice; I do not see her" (Woolf, 1985, p. 81). She concludes: "I suppose that I did for myself what psycho-analysts do for their patients. I expressed some very long felt and deeply felt emotion. And in expressing it I explained it and then laid it to rest." (*ibid.*) So this early 20th century woman writer could lay her ghosts by writing experimental novels, but what about you and me?

There is a spectrum of work on writing in the UK, from writing for personal development (Hunt & Sampson, 1998, 2005; Hunt, 2000), through personal and professional development for helping professionals in their work (Bolton, 2005; Bolton et al, 2004), to therapeutic writing for people wanting to address specific personal issues (Bolton, 1999). A great deal of practical wisdom exists in the area of teaching and facilitating writing in all these forms. These may not always be available to practitioners who focus mainly on talking therapy, however, so it is useful that a resource book has recently appeared to help with developing writing practice, running workshops and activities (Bolton et al, 2006).

Writing as empowerment

It will be clear by now that writing can be used to extend referential contexts, both personal and in wider social systems. Writers can explore themselves in relation to issues, institutions and people in general and, better still, they can choose how much or how little they share with others. Children who bring their writing to sessions in the Child and Adolescent Mental Health Service where I work seem invariably to be walking a little taller when they leave the room. Parents can feel validated by recording their experiences, and therapists themselves can feel pretty good about writing a well crafted report. If this routine writing leads to new insights and the possibility of a more creative therapeutic encounter, then so much the better.

I was very impressed a few years ago at a conference attended by a variety of community writing groups. They presented projects, some of which were sponsored by local authorities or the Arts Council and some of which arose from groups of like-minded individuals coming together to find solidarity around a particular social issue. These writing projects used a range of languages, and some featured writing in several different languages simultaneously, so that children in multi-lingual social settings could experience collective involvement with each other. I was particularly taken with a project in which a group of East African women wrote, using both English and their mother tongues, about their experiences of migration and making a life in Yorkshire. After meeting them I presented some of their writing in the AFT magazine *Context* (Burns, 2000). Readers are likely to find writing groups somewhere in their own neighbourhood, possibly composed of people whose individual voices feel marginalised or even silenced. Writing often means finding and strengthening those voices, finding and keeping a place in a community.

The coincidence of literary inspiration and mental distress has a long history. Many writers, including some we have already mentioned, like Virginia Woolf and Sylvia Plath, have lived simul-taneously with outstanding creativity and profound mental dis-tress. The nature of the relationship between disposition and artistic production remains to be clarified. It is often characterised by an urgent search for self, a struggle (sometimes mortal) for survival and expression. The impulse to write, whilst undeniable, seems rarely to have been the route to relief. Kay Redfield Jamison explores this conundrum for herself and for others in her books *Touched with Fire: Manic-Depressive Illness and the Artistic Temperament* (1996) and *An Unquiet Mind: a Memoir of Moods and Madness* (1997). As a Pro-fessor of Psychiatry and a sufferer from manic-depressive illness, she writes with passion and clarity about the personal experience and the many examples of associated artistic genius. She begins by acknowledging: "That impassioned moods, shattered reason, and the artistic temperament can be welded into a 'fine madness' remains a fiercely controversial belief"(1996, p. 3).

The idea of a "fine madness" is also present in the historical col-lections of art works created by residents in psychiatric institutions, the Bethlem Hospital being one (www.bethlemheritage.org.uk). In 1997 the Bethlem and Maudsley Trust published a collection of poems entitled *Beyond Bedlam: Poems Written out of Mental Distress* (Smith & Sweeney, 1997). It contained poems by established poets and previously published writers like William Blake, Sylvia Plath, Anne Sexton, Jean "Binta" Breeze, John Clare, Robert Lowell and Emily Dickinson. Other contributions were sought through fly-ers and organisations such as Survivors' Poetry and the National

Schizophrenia Fellowship, and through poetry publications. Ten years later Magma Poetry Online (www.magmapoetry.com), a UK poetry magazine, has approached the living contributors to ask them for their recollections. Pascale Petit ("Frozen Falls", "Eisriesenwelt") said: "It was a coming out. The fact that the two editors were brilliant high-profile poets and that it was published by Anvil made it for the first time seem okay to write poems about mental distress." Mala Mason ("Survivor") said: "When I got my copy and saw my poem in it, I felt very elated. Now I knew that no matter how many times I might put myself down, I had something concrete to point to, to say 'yes, I have achieved something in my life which makes a mark in the world, and it will be there always'."

Writing as social enquiry: alternative writing in ethnography

Writing, then, is a powerful tool for personal exploration and growth, but it is also important for building our collective knowledge of what it is to be a social being. As is already clear, this can take many forms. One body of work which has impressed me is that of interpretive ethnographers (Denzin, 1997; Ellis & Bochner, 1996). This writing is rooted firmly in the soil of ethnography: the descriptions produced by researchers who venture into a particular social/cultural field, observing and recording what they find. It can also be so close to literature that there is a significant argument as to which is the better classification. This makes it a "liminal" or borderline activity. As we have discussed previously, this is a remarkably creative place to be.

Denzin uses the example of James Joyce's literary experimentation to inform his own journey from the kind of reality mapping which produces an impression of objective representations to the "contradictory, shifting, and fragile worlds" of embodied, subjective experience. This, he maintains, is what is required in the contemporary quest for understanding (1997, p. 25). Ellis and Bochner (1996), following a similar rationale, introduce just the sort of writing which looks at experience from the inside and recreates for the reader the combination of insider and outsider view which characterises the engagement with literary texts. Here, individual ethnographers write their own experience of states of being, like living with bulimia (Tillmann-Healey, 1996), surviving child sexual abuse and retelling the story alongside that of another survivor (Fox, 1996), caring for a parent whilst reflecting on becoming a parent (Ellis, 1996). The relationship of this writing with qualitative research is thought-provoking, but the power of the accounts included in this volume speaks for itself. It is the power to communicate.

Positioning the self: writing and reflexivity

"In the social sciences there is only interpretation. Nothing speaks for itself" (Denzin, 1998, p. 313). A few years ago I undertook a study of family therapists' (literary) reading and its impact on their development as clinical practitioners, from early in training through to the most senior positions in the profession (see also Chapter Five). I am looking at this here because it is my own direct experience of writing as part of a meaning-making exercise, involving self-exploration as well as dialogue with others. The study was exploratory and made use of a mixed methodology, including a Delphi study, interviews, and the analysis of a training group. Making sense of these disparate but related sources of data meant I had to collect information from each in turn, considering them individually and in relation to each other, constructing an interpretive map as I went along. The interpretive map was composed in and through the reading of the data and the writing of the explanatory text.

Qualitative research approaches do not presuppose an objective view of what can be found. In fact, the researcher is called upon to make explicit use of subjective experience to understand what he or she encounters, in very much the same way as participants in therapy do. As co-editor of the *Handbook of Qualitative Research*, Norman Denzin maintains that "methods of making sense of experience are always personal" and "one learns about method by thinking about how one makes sense of one's own life"(1998, p. 315). This means that researchers have to be very aware of how they position themselves, e.g. as participant, as interpreter. They assume different positions at different times, and they have to explain this as clearly as possible. Biases are expected, and influences on the interpretation must be accounted for. This enables the consumer of research findings to achieve an informed understanding of what has been done and what new knowledge may be available. In my study of family therapists' reading and its impact on their practice, I found a way of positioning myself to account for important influences on my enquiry and to explore the impact of my own literary reading on the activity in hand. I wrote a reflexive commentary mediated by several texts which I had found inspirational.

Writing is a key activity in the research process, not only because it offers a way for the researcher to be reflexive in the ways mentioned above, but because it stimulates the necessary thinking and engagement. Laurel Richardson proposes that writing is itself a method of enquiry (2000). This idea is the counterpart, in the world of qualitative research, of the notion that writing can play a vital part in the personal and interpersonal explorations of therapy. There are many parallels between qualitative research and therapy. Not the least of these is that both varieties of the quest for meaning can leave their proponents in situations of stress, bewilderment, and possibly even despair. In my case (as researcher), the incipient despair arose from finding myself with a mass of fascinating data and not knowing quite what to do with it to advance my search for knowledge. This is a little like the predicament of the therapists in Vignette 3 at the head of this chapter: they have intuitions and information but have not yet found a way to use them. Into this "dark night" of the intellect came the words of Norman Denzin to make me feel less alone: "Field workers can neither make sense of nor understand what has been learned until they sit down and write the interpretive text, telling the story first to themselves and then to their significant others and then to the public"(1998, p. 317). So I got on with the writing!

The idea of a "dark night of the soul" has inspired writers from the 16th century Spanish mystic St John of the Cross to 19th century poet Gerard Manley Hopkins. T.S. Eliot's *Four Quartets* draw directly on the words of St John of the Cross. These poems formed the basis of one part of my reflexive commentary. In therapy, in qualitative research, and in the activities of daily life, feeling at a loss can be disorientating and even disabling. The person can feel threatened, helpless and out of contact with their own abilities and potentials. It is a very common and even predictable feeling, though, when learning is taking place. As I read Eliot's words in "East Coker" ("In order to arrive at what you do not know/You must go by a way which is the way of ignorance") and wrote about them, incorporating them in my own interpretive text, I really began to feel their deep significance in my state of despair. It was appropriate that I felt at a loss because this, paradoxically, was the way to go!

My own experience of writing (and writing about reading) as a method of personal positioning was very persuasive, drawing more than a little, I now think, on the kinds of ideas which inspired Penn and Frankfurt in their thinking about "participant texts". The act of writing enabled me to reveal meanings that were otherwise invisible and to explore completely new pathways to significance. It was helpful in achieving a reflexive position in relation to my research, and in helping me to withstand the destructive forces of discouragement and confusion.

Conclusion

This chapter has looked at writing from a number of viewpoints, starting with some everyday scenarios chosen pretty much at random from the array of writing situations in our complex world. Writing itself is a physical act which externalises states of mind and internal processes which are otherwise invisible to others. It is also part of a dialogue, whether internal only or involving the voices of others. It is always embedded in a social context. Both reading and writing are invaluable aids in therapy training and continuing professional development.

I have tried to put up a number of signposts which will, I hope, be helpful to readers who want to follow up any of the areas I have touched upon. The subject is huge and resists synthesis in a small chapter like this, so readers are encouraged to pursue topics which interest them. Some of this pursuit is relatively energy-efficient as the internet is full of writing, and writing about writing. There are also many people and groups which are just waiting to welcome people who, for example, want to do some writing for their own personal and professional development. I haven't mentioned LAPIDUS (www.lapidus.org.uk) until now in this chapter, but if you're interested in writing and meeting up with other writers, this is the place for you. It is a UK-based organisation, now ten years old, which exists "to promote healing and personal growth through writing and reading". Members are drawn from all areas of health and social care, academia and the general writing public.

Of course you really can do writing completely on your own, and that is what some people love about it, but it is so much better with others.

Exercise: Several ways to get writing!

PART III

ARE WE NEARLY THERE?

CHAPTER SEVEN

Destinations and endings

"What might have been and what has been
Point to one end, which is always present."
(T.S. Eliot, "Burnt Norton", 1935)

This book has set out to represent a journey of exploration. We have been investigating the proposition that literary resources may complement and enrich therapeutic approaches and augment the available range of personal skills and therapeutic techniques. If we follow the journey metaphor, then this concluding chapter has to say something about the destination. In true reflective style, it also has to say a few things about the journey and pick up any unresolved items we may have dropped along the way.

Readers may be asking, "are we nearly there yet?" Like many questions commonly asked by fractious children, this one, though relevant, may be difficult to answer. Usually travellers are keen to reach their destination, as long as it is not the kind of "Final Destination" depicted in a recent series of horror films and related novels. In these, a group of innocents cheat death the first time around, but are neatly picked off, one at a time, in due course. This is a kind of battle with fate, an alarming analogy for readers entering the home stretch.

We can rest assured, however, that this journey is not approaching any "final" conclusion. Like all good endings, it will leave many more goals and pathways to be explored. These "forward destinations" are those which we could not have foreseen or might not have been so interested in at the outset. A good novel will leave us keen for more at the end of every chapter. Writers, from Charles Dickens, Leo Tolstoy and Daphne du Maurier to Stephen King, have given us splendid examples of the "page turner" or "unputdownable" book which is captivating, seriously thought-provoking, and "literary". The term "literary" tends to suggest that the work will be predominantly concerned with ideas and will be expressed in a special kind of language, mostly to distinguish it from "popular" writing. We have defined "literary" according to the effect produced in relationship with the reader: stimulation for the imagination; a sense of relevance in social life as it exists; the power to open up different possibilities; multiplicity of interpretation; the propensity to link senses, emotions, and intellect. Sometimes, as in the qualitative research which generated the "literature and therapy" project, "literary" was just what participants produced when asked to find a "literary extract". The only criteria were that it should have some significance for their current concerns and be suitable for discussion with others. Literary activities and practices are, above all, about meaning-making in personal and shared lives. This simple definition has fuelled our journey and kept us curious.

In the kind of book which offers these literary prizes, the last page of all needs to leave us satisfied but thoughtful, our curiosity merely resting to enjoy where we have got to while it starts planning the next trip. Like a satisfying ending in therapy, the last page is likely to take us back to the beginning, but show it to us in such a way that we can "know the place for the first time" (Eliot, "Little Gidding", 1944). We'll return to this later.

Where we started

Initially, we set out to examine a view of therapists' development and the nature of the therapeutic relationship, through the medium of literary texts and practices like reading and writing. This medium is characterised by the use of external reference points which are culturally, and personally, significant. The business of *Literature and Therapy: a Systemic View* has not been to introduce a new therapeutic method but to alert us all to the possibilities inherent in taking an approach which:

- gives due weight to the art of therapy and values the aesthetics, or form, of activities which flow from the conscious and critical use of literary resources;
- promotes a multilayered notion of therapy which makes active use of the emotions and the senses and includes informed intuition as part of therapeutic engagement;
- goes some way to redress the inevitable imbalance of power in therapeutic relationships, by the use of texts (poems, novels etc.) as reference points which are equally available to all participants;
- recognises the value of indeterminacy in human affairs, helps us to work with our own "not knowing", and prompts us to seek richness in uncertainty;
- takes every opportunity to explore the metaphors, both overt and hidden, which shape our thinking, with a view to finding new perspectives and productive but hitherto unnoticed or invisible pathways;
- recognises the value of playfulness and is not afraid to go for it;
- promotes reflection (pondering) and reflexivity: the recognition of our own part in what happens around us, and the ability to transform realities by changing ourselves.

A few years ago I developed a hunch that ways of reading literature had much in common with contemporary talking therapy approaches. This vague idea grew as I revisited "literary" ways of reading and found that not only did books I used to know give me particular insights, but the ways I engaged with them were either directly transferable to, or gave me ideas about, the work I could do with families and individuals.

Travelling with the mariner

To give an example, one of my favourite poems, Coleridge's *The Rime of the Ancient Mariner,* is itself a journey of exploration through human motivations and particularly the push and pull of destructive impulses. When I ask myself why the poem attracts me and feels relevant in my personal and professional life, the answer is that it entices and compels me to follow the mariner's voyage, watching his actions with their fearful consequences, and the struggle he has to make amends. It is not just observation, though. I feel I am inside the action; but at the same time can move between "insider" and "outsider" positions (see *Literature—why bother?* in Chapter Two). The poem creates a powerful emotional bond with me and becomes my own subjective experience. Reading it is both cathartic (gives expression to, and release from, emotional tensions) and helps me to construct a metaphorical framework for achieving peace and resolution. The makings of an experiential lesson in personal growth are there in the text, but the reader has the option to accept or reject them. Ultimately, what is created in the reading is always personal and unique.

As a reader, I engage with the story, the emotions and the spiritual/philosophical questions it poses. It is a catalyst for development. I give it my fullest attention, commit myself to it body and mind, and carry it with me long after the reading is over. In return, my own understandings and feelings are transformed. Just like the wedding guest, who (in the manner of a therapist) is selected by the mariner to witness the narrative of his experience, the reader is likely to be "sadder" and "wiser" by the close of the last stanza. In therapy, and family therapy in particular, participants witness each other's engagement with the stories and the experiences which belong to their own unique, shared journey. They are often sadder during the course of the work and hope to be wiser at its conclusion.

Reading as a metaphor for therapy?

The suggestion that reading might become a powerful metaphor for therapy is advanced in earlier chapters. If this proposition is to be accepted, there are a few points to be re-examined critically now that we have nearly reached the end of our exploration. The obvious point is that the two are dissimilar in many ways. Therapy happens in conversation between people in real time, while reading is a solitary activity which can be picked up and put down over a variable period. The text of a novel or poem is fixed on the page, whereas that created in a therapy session is in the air. It is ephemeral, unless captured and transcribed verbatim, as in a research situation, or in summary by the writing of a letter or some kind of participant text (Penn & Frankfurt, 1994). The point is that metaphors work by juxtaposing ostensibly unrelated things, drawing out existing qualities which may be hidden, whilst suggesting the generation of new perceptions and insights. Therapy and reading are clearly not the same activity but they are mutually illuminating.

As the writer who is approaching the conclusion of a journey, I have discovered that wholehearted dialogical engagement with a text is fundamental to transformations of meaning, be it the written text of a poem or the spoken text of a therapy session. This is the underlying quality which binds them together. The reader is engaged through literary tropes (use of language, selection of images, emotional tone etc.) and the general resonance of the subject matter; the therapist through similar phenomena, with the addition of visual and other sensory factors. Engagement is a similar process, consisting of a circular (mutual) relationship between all parties (reader, writer, therapist, clients) with, and through, the interpretive text they create between them. Indeterminacies which draw the reader in are key to involvement with literary texts. Therapeutic conversations are characterised by attention to inconsistencies and gaps in narratives, purposeful introduction of open questions and exploration of alternative viewpoints. Literary reading induces a frame of mind which is at once intensely concentrated and open to the possibilities generated by the poem or the story. This is the poet Keats's notion of "negative capability" (1817). It also gives rise to "that willing suspension of disbelief" (Coleridge, 1817, Chapter XIV) which enables the reader both to participate in the experience and to stand outside it. The prospect of harnessing these two qualities alone in the service of therapy would seem to justify the adoption of this metaphor. The analogy between reading and therapy is not a simple fit, but it is a thought- (and feeling-) provoking one, and that is what counts.

I hope that readers of this book will be in a position to recognise many forward destinations for themselves and will be emboldened to use the juxtaposition of literature and therapy in creative ways which add to their practice. For me, the main pleasure and stimulus lies in exploring specific texts and following where they lead, in the confidence that I will learn something salient about myself as a person and a therapist. What I learn is part of what I offer when

I am working as a therapist, that is, it becomes part of the "self" I use as a therapeutic tool. This learning combines both head and heart, because literature always demands a balance of attention to both. Above all, it fuels me up to go on.

A perilous journey?

As the Ancient Mariner had reason to know, even the most innocent-seeming trips can turn into a nightmare for all concerned. Families may come to our services hoping for one thing and get something quite different. Individuals may discover unwelcome things about themselves or their nearest and dearest. Therapists may (and usually do) set out with high hopes of their ability to help. Colleagues can have very lofty expectations of each other, especially if they have to rely on each other in the stressful context of face-to-face contact with their clientele. Supervisees look to their supervisors for support and wisdom, and can be very disappointed if this relationship proves limited. Since this is the last chapter, we need to look at some endings which are potentially (or actually) unhappy.

Here are a couple of possible situations.

Vignette 1

The scene is a medium sized room in a community Child and Adolescent Mental Health Service. There is a circle of easy chairs, and in them sit the parents and daughter we first saw in the waiting room back at the beginning of Chapter One. You may remember the woman, elegantly casual but looking tired and drawn, the father in the smart suit, and the fourteen-year-old girl in baggy clothing.

They have been joined in the room by a family therapist, a robust looking man in his early forties, and a young female psychiatrist. They have been discussing the worries which have brought the family to the Clinic. It seems that the girl, Charlotte, is having problems with friends at school, and her academic work is gradually losing the excellence it used to show. The mother, Sally, is worried about her daughter's performance in her upcoming exams, and about the impact of all the anxiety thus created on her younger two children. The father, Ted, works long hours in his City solicitors' office and is rarely, if ever, available to lend a hand at home. He does try, however, to keep appointments at school and other important places. He feels under immense pressure at work, and has just said it is unlikely that he will be able to come to another appointment at the Clinic unless it can be made before 9 am or after 5 pm. The girl sits quietly with her head bowed while her mother and father engage in a lively, verging on heated, discussion of the rights and wrongs of the situation.

The family therapist finally gets a word in to ask if this is typical of the kind of interchange they would have at home, and if so, how they go about reaching a mutually acceptable conclusion. He goes on to ask what the parents remember about how such questions were resolved when they were young teenagers in their respective families.

By way of answer, Dad does not know how things were worked out because he was at boarding school from the age of eight. Mum thinks hers was just an ordinary happy family and differences of opinion simply did not occur.

A short while later, the young psychiatrist asks about Charlotte's general health, and her weight in particular. At this point a hush falls over the group. The therapist has the strong impression that each party to the conversation is struggling with the impulse to leave the room.

Vignette 2

The scene is the same room, in the same agency, but with a different group of people. This time there are only adults present: an angry looking man with his partner, who looks as though she would like to sink through the floor; a family therapist in her early thirties who has been working with the family of the angry looking man; an elegant, grey haired Child Psychotherapist who has been working for a year and a half with the angry man's twelve-year-old son, Joe; the two therapists' line manager. The manager is present as the representative of the therapists' employing Trust.

The story is as follows: both the family therapist and the individual therapist have become increasingly concerned about the way in which Joe's contact arrangements with his father are being handled. Joe's parents are divorced. His mother, who has asked not to be included in this meeting, claims she is intimidated by her ex-husband and is increasingly worried about insisting that Joe go to his father on alternate weekends. She is not sure that there is any physical risk for Joe. It is mostly that she feels undermined by her ex-husband's constant criticism, and for her, Joe's contact visits keep this troublesome relationship alive. The family therapist has tried to raise these questions with Joe's mother and father jointly, without success. He has, therefore, been considering how far it is appropriate to define the situation as one of Child Protection and refer to the local Social Services agency. Joe has two much younger half-siblings, who live with their mother and their father, her current partner.

Joe's father has made a complaint to the two therapists' employer about what he sees as the aspersions they are casting on him, his abilities as a parent, and his character in general. He proposes to pursue this complaint with a view to discontinuing Joe's therapy. The Child Psychotherapist thinks this would be a personal disaster for Joe.

These two brief stories exemplify situations in which some, or all, participants in therapeutic work wish they had never started in the first place. All have embarked upon a journey which promises pain and danger as well as the possibility of healing. At this stage in the book, readers will not expect a literary text to be prescribed for each situation. Our approach has been much more to look to literary texts, and our readings of them, to act a bit like a systemic fertiliser, promoting our sensitivities and empathic abilities, both particular and general. "Prescriptions" can, of course, be given to good effect, as bibliotherapists have shown (Gold, 2001), and the approach we have been exploring would not oppose this where it fits.

In Vignette 1, for example, Ted might well feel he has things in common with Odysseus, the eponymous hero of Homer's *Odyssey*, who also features in the *Iliad*. Odysseus (Ulysses in Latin) fights in the Trojan War and then wanders through many adventures and perils, returning after 20 years to his home in Ithaca disguised as a beggar and unrecognised by everyone apart from his dog. Ted's position in the family is simultaneously central and peripheral. He may not feel he can measure up to what is expected of him. He may also feel unrecognised and unappreciated so that he stays away more, compounding the negativity with which he is viewed, and with which he views himself. Sally may envy his apparent freedom, and feel justified in casting him out of the intimate areas of family life. The therapist could decide to explore these themes, with or without reference to the many adventures which kept Odysseus busy for the 20 years on his way home after the war. If the story resonates for the therapists and/or the family, new areas of interest may suggest themselves, like the relationships outside the family which consume Ted's energy and distract him from, or substitute for, those within it.

Looking at things a little differently, on the Ancient Greek theme, family members might also trace similarities between their own situation and that of the family of Agamemnon, another hero of Homer's *Iliad*. He offers his daughter Iphigenia as a sacrifice for victory during the course of the Trojan War. On his return home, he is murdered by his wife, Clytemnestra, and her lover, Aegisthus. They then go on to reign over his kingdom. These stories gave rise to many ancient Greek tragic dramas, notably the *Oresteia* of Aeschylus and the Electra plays of Sophocles and Euripides, in which Agamemnon's children seek to counteract the wrongs done by their parents. It is easy to see how their dark and bloody content could dramatise the questions which preoccupy all the members of our first family. Their 21st century issues may well be those of life and death. There is marital disharmony and a sense that the family has been abandoned by its most apparently powerful member. Parents feel at a loss to know how to resolve the situation because their own relational repertoires were impoverished in their early lives. Charlotte's health is a no-go area for direct concern, and she may be occupying a "sacrificial" role, partly from her own choice and partly because it is the price of domestic peace and/or public success. A group of siblings stand by as horrified observers of the parents' actions, compelled to inaction in the present but storing up all manner of trouble and anguish for the future. If the therapy session reaches a crescendo of discomfort with the broaching of Charlotte's possible eating disorder, it is because this is the way the family drama is structured. It is the moment of unbearable tension and the naming of the unnameable.

This is just one interpretation, of course, but one which makes some sense and flows from the story of Agamemnon and the house of Atreus. Greek tragedies were designed to mirror and explore personal flaws and the brutal and violent sides of human behaviour in the most striking and terrifying ways. Spectators were led to experience the catharsis we mentioned earlier in the chapter. In this way, the more noble, beautiful and, we might say, healthy aspects were enabled to re-assert themselves, not only on the stage but in the consciousness of the audience. No prescriptions are on offer here, and certainly no quick answers. There are signposts, however, even if they are pointing down some of the steeper and stonier paths which have to be trodden if healing and reconciliation are to be possible.

The journey of therapy can also be full of pitfalls for therapists, as Vignette 2 reminds us. In addition to the significance for the families involved, this situation could feel like the final straw for a hard pressed professional. Therapeutic engagements are fragile and deeply invested with emotional energy on both sides. It is one thing to accept that we are all "wounded" in one way or another and that the particular nature of a therapist's wounds has significance as part of the therapeutic process. Nevertheless, an incapacitated or burnt-out therapist can bring little which is serviceable into a therapeutic engagement. Complaints, whether formal or informal, undermine the confidence of even the most experienced practitioners, making them question their competence and even their own motivations. It is hard to receive complaints positively in therapy, even when they are about external factors and brought to the therapist as part of a wide-ranging therapeutic discussion (O'Reilly, 2005; Glover, 2005). Negative feelings are naturally the stuff of therapy, but formal complaints about a clinician or multidisciplinary group take this into a different frame, damaging the sense of "self" which is vital for therapists who have to work through empathy and the creation of shared subjectivities. Organisations and teams may have excellent systems for managing the stress involved, or they may not.

Reading your way through stress

Ultimately negativity is experienced subjectively and must be addressed personally. It may not be exaggerating to suggest that a person who is the subject of a complaint might wake up feeling quite different from his or her normal self, rather like Gregor Samsa, who, on waking from an anxious dream one morning "discovered that in bed he had been changed into a monstrous verminous bug" (Kafka, *Metamorphosis*). The experience is disorientating and is likely to make the subject feel threatened. Simply recognising one's own situation in a book can be supportive and affirming. Maybe the story can offer new perspectives, and the mysterious processes of language will lift the reader into a different frame of mind where other possibilities can be spotted. Given what we have learned about how our lives can be influenced by those we follow in books or on the TV, a vulnerable-feeling person might well turn to epics of suffering and survival: Steinbeck's *Grapes of Wrath*; Mitchell's *Gone with the Wind*; the true stories of *Alive* by Piers Paul Read and Joe Simpson's story, *Touching the Void*; Anne Michaels' *Fugitive Pieces* or Primo Levi's *If This is a Man*. If these are too romantic or too harrowing, what about *The Shipping News* by Annie Proulx, Maya Angelou's *I Know Why the Caged Bird Sings* or Alice Walker's *The Color Purple*? A book does not have to fit the reader and the circumstances exactly to give help in times of high emotion and feeling lost. Seamus Deane's *Reading in the Dark* confronts the dangers and passionate contradictions of surviving in troubled times. The reader does not have to have grown up in 1950s Derry to feel this book's power and benefit from its insights. In fact, we know that holes in the story and mismatches with the reader's experience are essential to engagement. They stimulate us to fill in the missing parts with relevant elements from our own lives. For example, if someone is feeling victimised, revisiting *Jane Eyre*, the story of a nineteenth century governess, can be a potent reminder that simply being persecuted and having bad experiences do not oblige a person actually to become a victim.

What is helpful for someone under acute emotional stress varies with taste, and from person to person, but we have reason to think that the emotional "feel" is crucially important. Reading something quite different, and apparently nothing to do with the cause of the stress, may be just what is needed to restore a sense of perspective. Certain genres, or predominantly formulaic (so-called "escapist") literature may suggest themselves, like romance, science fiction, detective fiction, or gothic novels. It is essential that individuals follow their own intuition. It has been said that "a little of what you fancy does you good", and music hall artiste Marie Lloyd's assertion has a lot to be said for it in these circumstances. Gothic-type novels, for example, can be expected to feature settings and events which inspire, or invite the reader to observe, terror. Stock characters include "tyrants", "villains", "persecuted maidens", "madwomen", "monsters", "demons" and so on. These are not everyone's cup of tea by any means, but the point is that characters, events and predicaments may be seen as imaginative constructions of the kinds of stresses we have been considering. Wandering amongst them in relative safety may offer ideal conditions for "exorcising" their malevolent influences.

Undoubtedly, many people confronted with crises in personal or professional life would turn to song lyrics for inspiration. It is not for nothing that Gloria Gaynor's "I Will Survive" has achieved anthem status with many disparate groups. Songs, both lyrics and music, would fill a whole (different) book. Suffice to say that to be helpful, there needs to be some element of resonance in narrative, imagery or emotional tone which captures the imagination, enables the reader or listener to share the experience from both insider and outsider positions, and promotes a different relationship with the cause of their discomfort. Songs are particularly good for hard pressed professionals because they can be accessed easily, hummed almost any time, and, perhaps most important of all, can be played over and over whilst driving.

Exploring "the dark side"

Since therapists tend to be sensitive and self-questioning types, it is likely that they will want to examine their own part in whatever may have been difficult or bruising in their work. This is not only ethically important, and a prescribed stance for family therapists and other practitioners of a systemic persuasion, it can also be surprisingly stimulating and even refreshing. Conversations with supervisors and colleagues, and taking feedback from clients, are obviously essential, but this is also a personal matter, and reading may be able to access aspects of ourselves which other approaches cannot readily reach. Participants in the study I have described at points throughout this book found that approaching their development though formative literary texts was very evocative emotionally.

There is every chance that contemplating our own "dark sides", through a method which is essentially playful, can be both life-saving and entertaining. After all, standing on the bright side and looking at the dark side is the basis of much that is enjoyable in literature and film. The serious aspect of self examination is undeniable, but literature can make extra positions available and give more room for manoeuvre. This kind of play is similar to the experiential "practising" which has been advocated elsewhere for readers. For example, a reading of Ian McEwan's *Saturday* or *Enduring Love* would help the reader to explore aspects of stalking and being harassed, including the shifting patterns of personal responsibility which operate in complex situations. It would also allow the reader to marvel at the ease with which the viewpoint can shift in the hands of the novelist, and the facility with which different perspectives can be adopted by the reader. Nothing is as fixed as it seems.

R.L. Stevenson's story *The Strange Case of Dr Jekyll and Mr Hyde* is a well-known exploration of the duality, or indeed multiplicity, of human nature:

> I thus drew steadily nearer to that truth by whose partial discovery I have been doomed to such a dreadful shipwreck: that man is not truly one, but truly two. I say two because the state of my knowledge does not pass beyond that point... I hazard the guess that man will ultimately be known for a mere polity of multifarious, incongruous and independent denizens.

Jekyll and Hyde are doubles, Jekyll having the monopoly of good characteristics and Hyde personifying the long denied evil side. Initially Hyde seems rather puny, small and young, but gradually he gains in strength and malevolence. The novel ends with Jekyll relinquishing his hold on life, as Hyde has gained the upper hand and effectively banished his better half. It is notable that though ultimately loathsome, Hyde is said to be the "livelier", and Jekyll admits that he finds his alter ego seductive. He manages to express aspects of personality, like anger, which had not previously been acknowledged, and this is gratifying from the outset. Once the genie is out of the bottle there is no possibility of reverse, however, and Hyde grows increasingly monstrous and dangerous. He no longer appears only when summoned. He, and his actions, cannot be contained.

We all have a "dark side" which we ignore at our peril. Jekyll's experiment is potentially deadly. It has the power to change the shape and size of his body as well as his personality. This is what he seeks, but the experiment also has the power to kill, to "utterly blot out that immaterial tabernacle which I looked to it to change". Flirting with the "dark side" is dangerous, but it can also reveal nuances of identity which hitherto we barely knew existed. Taking the journey of exploration with Jekyll's friend Utterson allows the reader to play with the possibilities and venture cautiously into the danger zone. Utterson, the observer, cannot get the images of Jekyll's transformation out of his head. They pass through his mind like "a scroll of lighted pictures". He is enslaved by curiosity and a desire to know more about the figure of his visions. The reader is drawn inexorably by the way the full horror is revealed, little by little, from multiple viewpoints.

Carl Jung described the phenomenon of the "Wounded Healer" in the unconscious relationship between analyst and patient, and warned of its dangers as well as its necessity (Jung 1989). Maybe it is also time to pay some attention to the "Jekyll and Hyde" healer and the risks and strengths of working with the "dark side".

"He's just a Jekyll and Hyde"

In the Child and Adolescent Mental Health Service where I work, therapists are often called upon to exercise their curiosity about the quality of children's behaviour. Parents say: "he's a real Jekyll and Hyde", and I suppose that is why Stevenson's story is such a popular one. The image of a sudden and terrifying metamorphosis is so striking, especially when it is thought to be inexplicable. There are all kinds of variations on this theme, one of which is given here.

Vignette 3

> Like the family in Vignette 1, this trio have been waiting since Chapter One, although this session is on a later day.
>
> The mother, Sarah, has brought her two boys Andrew (8) and Austin (6) to see the therapist because Andrew's behaviour is so

difficult at home. One minute he is quiet, polite and amenable, she says. The next he is screaming, swearing and hitting out at anyone who happens to be in the way. It is like turning on a switch. He never used to be like this. Never, that is, until about five months ago.

What happened then?

Well, that was a hard time. The boys' grandmother died. She was their family rock and was the one person who kept them going after the boys' father moved on.

At this point Sarah's eyes fill with tears and both boys move to her side.

Andrew's behaviour is especially hard to bear because everyone is so sad and bereft. Sarah feels she cannot cope, and Austin is becoming very upset and frightened. It also seems very unfair that Andrew has none of these "fits" when in school.

The therapist asks more about how the grandmother used to help.

She used to look after the boys so that Sarah could go to work. They all enjoyed her cooking and her home, which she had made seem just like a home in Jamaica, where she lived when she was a girl.

Austin says that what he liked best of all was that his grandma used to tell them stories: special Jamaican stories about a tricky little spider creature called Anancy.

The therapist knows only a little about Anancy but is always willing to ask. Sarah remembers the stories from her own childhood, although she hasn't thought of them for years. Thinking about her mum cuddled up with the boys, telling them what she remembers as rather subversive and naughty stories, lights up her face with a smile. She thinks Anancy was quite resourceful and could often find a way out of difficult situations.

The therapist thinks that there may be many hard days to come for the little family. There are no easy solutions for boys who can suddenly flip from Mr Nice Guy to a monster. This behaviour signals that there is a serious problem somewhere, and such problems are not usually susceptible to simple remedies. If things do not improve quickly Andrew will also get a bad name, and that is very hard to shake off. Nevertheless, with Anancy on hand to help, the situation does not look so bleak. There are stories to read and listen to, and to retell. It is possible that Sarah will rediscover some of the fun of telling these stories to her own children, and in doing so find herself a little closer to her beloved mother.

This Vignette highlights the importance of starting with what is being offered by the family. Although "Jekyll and Hyde" has passed into the language as a cliché denoting a recognisable kind of situation, and although we may see that the book itself can offer a more subtle understanding, this is not what most people have in mind. TV and film adaptations have tended to focus only on Jekyll's account, without the interior conversation which explores the depths of his internal conflict. These simplified versions are useful in themselves, however, introducing the idea that two or more contradictory aspects can co-exist in the same person and that some coherent motivation is at work. This notion is the driving force for the Incredible Hulk, in TV and film versions. It is also present in multi-dimensional romps like *Bill and Ted's Bogus Journey*, a 1991 film in which the clueless pair is pursued through time by hostile versions of themselves: the "evil usses". These are entertaining and possibly concept-expanding variations, but they leave more provocative questions of personal responsibility entirely untouched. Stevenson's text does provide a basis for contemplating personal transformations—both acceptable and the reverse.

Anancy stories may not necessarily contain the same motif, but they are about resourcefulness and surviving through difficult times. Andrew's behaviour is understandable as communication about the plight of his family, as well as personal grief. If Sarah can feel better and stronger, maybe through reconnecting with some of her own mother's resilience and love for her, then life for the two little boys will feel more secure. Andrew may learn a thing or two about confronting hardship. They can all find a common focus which is both meaningful and fun. Not least may be the access that Anancy can give to a cultural heritage and collective wisdom about living in times of trouble.

This figure exists in West African traditions as well as in the Caribbean. Trickster figures are common cultural motifs from Lilith to Bugs Bunny. The idea of shape-shifting (werewolves, or vampire stories, notably *Dracula* and *I am Legend*) may also be helpful in exploring the notion that a person can encompass contradictory qualities and behaviours. They also have the advantage of appealing to older children and adolescents. All these stories and literary treatments tend to problematise superficial or insensitive judgements, and open up discussion. If chosen and introduced with care, they can encourage participants to engage more fully in difficult conversations.

The last page: literary endings

We are now nearly at the end of our last chapter, and it is the moment to try and provide you, the reader, with a satisfactory conclusion which leaves you pondering what you have read and keen to try out new ideas. We have been talking about how literary reading can enrich lives, both directly and through therapeutic processes. Endings in therapy can be tough to achieve and painful to live through. At the same time they can be joyful and affirming affairs and/or sometimes a relief for all concerned. Like the idea of a "good death", the perception of a good ending is very much in the eye of the beholder. I would like to reflect briefly on a few favourites of mine in the hope that these will call to mind some of yours.

The examples I have chosen are rather random. I am following the lead of my intuition, very much in the way that the participants in groups I have described followed theirs, by browsing my bookshelves and picking whatever seems to call to me at the time. I have come to rely on this as a helpful technique, rather like following apparently random sequences in a kind of free association. One small and rather battered leather bound volume came to light in this way. It was a collection of John Milton's poetical works, which I bought at a jumble sale when I was at school. At that time I thought Milton's poetic voice was both majestic and subtly emotive, and I still do.

A grand finale

Milton was a poet in the grand manner, much influenced by the Classics in general and, in this case, the Roman poet Virgil in particular. He was a scholar and was also politically and scientifically aware. He was Secretary for Foreign Tongues in Oliver Cromwell's government, and visited Galileo whilst the latter was under house arrest on account of his "heretical" views on the motion of the Earth around the sun. Milton's works are not particularly fashionable at present, and I had not looked at them for a number of years. Handling this little book immediately took me back to the time when I was very keen on Milton and wanted to be a literature scholar myself. I looked at the endings of two epic (narrative) poems, *Samson Agonistes* and *Paradise Lost*.

Paradise Lost is the story of the war in Heaven, in which, incidentally, Satan gets the star part and all the best lines. It tells of the fall of Adam and Eve from grace and their expulsion from the Garden of Eden. The last lines are both poignant and expansive. In the belief system which informed Milton, and continues to inform the world's three monotheistic religions, Adam and Eve were poetic embodiments of our ancestors:

> The world was all before them, where to choose
> Their place of rest, and Providence their guide.
> They, hand in hand, with wandering steps and slow,
> Through Eden took their solitary way.

This, then, was Milton's ending for the beginning of the human race. Adam and Eve are on their own, sad for what they have lost, but looking forward to the kind of Paradise they can create between them: the first family. We know, and Milton did too, that leaving the protection of Eden would leave them exposed to endless replication of the feuding and fighting described between God and Satan, Angels, Archangels and so on. This ending touches us gently but also calls on us to exercise just that degree of awareness which has made Adam and Eve human.

Samson Agonistes, written within a few years of *Paradise Lost*, seems to me to have a more personal resonance. Samson, an Israelite hero, falls from grace by disobeying the commandment given by God. He loses his gift of superhuman physical strength. He is captured, blinded and humiliated by the Philistines, before pulling down the temple of the heathen god Dagon around their ears. It is said to be a discussion of, and reflection on, the question of predestination versus free will, an issue of great importance for 17th century Protestants in Europe. The wider context translates easily into 21st century terms, with its focus on personal responsibility and accountability in the face of persecution and coercion. Milton himself had been blind for many years by the time the poem was completed. The poetic drama is also a reflection on the expression, through suffering, of spiritual strength and enlightenment. To a contemporary reader, it would seem to have autobiographical significance.

The final words, which are spoken by the chorus, refer to the huge spiritual and emotional experience which the characters, and particularly Samson, have undergone. Peace and consolation are now possible: "And calm of mind, all passion spent".

It may be an effort for us, in the 21st century, to relate to the massive scale of Milton's works, and to his grounding in classical and religious myths and legends. The words here are simple, though, and eloquently express the outcome of mental and physical suffering when the heat of the moment is past. The calm of mind is both individual and collective. The passions are recognisable all around us on scales from global to domestic. Sometimes it is helpful to have a sense of the magnitude of the "passions" we may encounter in our lives, and the lives of those we work with. It helps us to contextualise what we do.

Something more mystical

Eliot's *Four Quartets* ("Burnt Norton", "East Coker", "The Dry Salvages" and "Little Gidding") have been much quoted recently in family therapy places. If I am honest, this choice is hardly random at all, as these poems call out to me whenever I see or hear them. I used them, along with "The Lady of Shalott", *Howards End* and *To the Lighthouse*, to construct a reflexive commentary to accompany the qualitative research project on which I have drawn during the course of this book. The meditations on beginnings and endings seem to fit very well with the "circular epistemology" on which family systems theory and practice are based. The poems are full of references to the cyclical nature of experience and the mysteries of time:

> Time present and time past
> Are both perhaps present in time future
> And time future contained in time past.
>   —T.S. Eliot, "Burnt Norton", 1935

Eliot's poetry, like Milton's, can be very erudite and full of references to knowledge which the reader may not possess. I find *Four Quartets* quite different, however. If the poems seem perplexing, it is because we have not yet entered into their way of thinking. It used to be said that the biggest task for people training to be family therapists was to achieve fluency in "systems thinking". Once that was done (and it did seem to happen suddenly, at an identifiable point), there was no turning back. You couldn't any more see individuals divorced from their relational context; you couldn't give much credit to linear-type communications which were not embedded in what came before and what came after. You couldn't fail to want to "connect" and to see patterns everywhere. You learned to talk and ask questions in ways that reflected this awareness, and the solutions you envisaged in therapy were ones that fitted with this "epistemology". Things have changed and diversified since I began to be interested in working with families in the early 1980s, but I would be surprised if new recruits to the profession would disagree with these basic principles. *Four Quartets* tend to be quite abstract, but their ideas do, I think, fit very well with "systems thinking", especially with respect to patterning and connections. The context may be cosmic, but the small and familiar are also there.

We have talked a good deal, in the foregoing chapters, about the contribution literary reading can make to helping us expand and appreciate the range of our emotions. The last passage of the poem "Little Gidding" is full of images, not our own, but intensely evocative nonetheless. Poetic images speak directly to our emotions, not sentimentally, but in a way which touches us at the core of our being. I find the following lines both thought-provoking and profoundly moving, not least because they were chosen by trainees in one of the groups I have written about from time to time during the course of the book. These words expressed their sense of developing identities approaching the end of their training:

> We shall not cease from exploration
> And the end of all our exploring
> Will be to arrive where we started
> And know the place for the first time.
>
> —T.S. Eliot, "Little Gidding", 1942

An artistic ending

The time has come to be brief. This ending will speak for itself, although I will give some context and, yet again, own up to promoting texts which mean something to me.

Virginia Woolf wrote *To the Lighthouse* as a fictionalised exploration of her own parents, and, hence, her relationship with their memory. The novel is experimental in form and attempts to explore inner psychological states in language. We have visited the book several times in previous chapters.

Here, on the last page, we are again talking about images. One of the guests at the Ramsays' holiday house party is a woman called Lily Briscoe. She is there at the beginning and she is there again at the end, some years later, with the Great War and several family deaths in between. She is painting a picture and observing the family critically throughout. On the last page Lily Briscoe, on land, thinks that Mr Ramsay, his son James and daughter Cam have reached the Lighthouse at last. The truth of all sorts of things has finally been revealed, but not in our part of the picture. Lily turns to her own canvas, she recognises it as an "attempt at something". She fears it will be hung in an attic or destroyed:

> But what did that matter? She asked herself, taking up her brush again. She looked at the steps; they were empty; she looked at her canvas; it was blurred. With a sudden intensity, as if she saw it clear for a second, she drew a line there, in the centre. It was done; it was finished. Yes, she thought, laying down her brush in extreme fatigue, I have had my vision.

I, too, have had my vision for the time being, albeit a fragmented and partial one. It is the time to rest, even while surreptitiously casting an eye around for the next beckoning pathway.

REFERENCES

Anderson, H. & Goolishian, H. (1988). Human Systems as Linguistic Systems: Preliminary and Evolving Ideas about the Implications for Clinical Theory. *Family Process, 27*: 371–393.

Bachelard, G. (1969). *The Poetics of Space* (trans. M. Jolas). Boston, MA: Beacon Press, 1994.

Bachelard, G. (1988). *On Poetic Imagination and Reverie* (trans. C. Gaudin). Woodstock, CT: Spring Publications.

Bacigalupe, G. (1996). Writing in Therapy: a Participatory Approach. *Journal of Family Therapy, 18*: 361–373.

Bateson, G. (1972). *Steps to an Ecology of Mind.* New York: Ballantine Books.

Bateson, G. (1979). *Mind in Nature: A Necessary Unity.* New York: Bantam Books.

Bennett, A. (1994). *Writing Home.* London: Faber & Faber.

Bloom, H. (1998). *Shakespeare: the Invention of the Human.* London: Fourth Estate.

Bolton, G. (1999). *The Therapeutic Potential of Creative Writing.* London: Jessica Kingsley.

Bolton, G. (2005). *Reflective Practice: Writing and Professional Development.* London: Sage.

Bolton, G., Howlett, S., Lago, C. & Wright, J.K. (2004). *Writing Cures: an Introductory Handbook of Writing in Counselling and Therapy.* Hove: Brunner-Routledge.

Bolton, G., Field, V. & Thompson, K. (2006). *Writing Works: A Resource Handbook for Therapeutic Writing Workshops and Activities.* London: Jessica Kingsley.

Bowen, B. & Robinson, G. (1998). *Therapeutic Stories: A Collection of Stories and Narrative Ideas.* Canterbury: AFT Publishing.

Bruner, J. (1986). *Actual Minds, Possible Worlds.* Cambridge, MA: Harvard University Press.

Bruner, J. (1990). *Acts of Meaning.* Cambridge, MA: Harvard University Press.

Burns, L. (2000). Shells on the Shore—Shells on a Woven Cord. *Context 47.*

Burns, L. (2003). *An Exploration of the Place of Literary Reading in Family Therapists' Personal and Professional Development.* Unpublished PhD thesis. Canterbury: Christchurch University.

Burns, L. & Kemps, C. (2002). Risky Business: the Rewards and Demands of Cross-Cultural Working with Colleagues. In: B. Mason & A. Sawyer (Eds.), *Exploring the Unsaid: Creativity, Risks and Dilemmas in Working Cross-Culturally.* London: Karnac.

Carey, J. (2005). *What Good are the Arts?* London: Faber & Faber.

Cecchin, G. (1987). Hypothesising, Circularity and Neutrality Revisited: an Invitation to Curiosity. *Family Process, 26:* 405–14.

Cecchin, G., Lane, G. & Ray, W. (1991). *Irreverence: a Strategy for Therapist Survival.* London: Karnac.

Charon, R. (2006). *Narrative Medicine: Honoring the Stories of Illness.* New York: Oxford University Press.

Coleridge, S.T. (1817). *Biographia Literaria.*

Cope, W. (1992). The Uncertainty of the Poet. In *Serious Concerns.* London: Faber & Faber.

Cox, M. (1992). *Shakespeare Comes to Broadmoor: The Actors Are Come Hither—The Performance of Tragedy in a Secure Psychiatric Hospital.* London: Jessica Kingsley.

Cox, M. & Theilgaard, A. (1994). *Shakespeare as Prompter: The Amending Imagination and the Therapeutic Process.* London: Jessica Kingsley.

Culler, J. (1997). What is Literature and Does it Matter? In: *Literary Theory: A Very Short Introduction.* Oxford: Oxford University Press.

Dallos, R. (1997). *Interacting Stories: Narratives, Family Beliefs and Therapy.* London: Karnac.

Dallos, R. (2007). *Attachment Narrative Therapy*. Maidenhead: Open University Press.

Dallos, R. & Trelfa, J. (1993). To Be or Not to Be: Family Beliefs, Madness and the Construction of Choice. *Journal of Family Psychotherapy*, 4: 63–82.

Damasio, A. (1999). *The Feeling of What Happens: Body, Emotion and the Making of Consciousness*. London: Heinemann.

Denzin, N. (1997). *Interpretive Ethnography: Ethnographic Practices for the 21st Century*. Thousand Oaks, CA: Sage.

Denzin, N. (1998). The Art and Politics of Interpretation. In: N. Denzin & Y. Lincoln (Eds.), *Handbook of Qualitative Research. Volume 3: Collecting and Interpreting Qualitative Materials*. Thousand Oaks, CA: Sage.

Eliot, T.S. (1920). *The Sacred Wood: Essays on Poetry and Criticism*. London: Faber & Faber, 1997.

Eliot, T.S. (1940). East Coker. In: *Four Quartets*. London: Faber & Faber, 2001.

Eliot, T.S. (1942). Little Gidding. In: *Four Quartets*. London: Faber & Faber, 2001.

Ellis, C. (1996). Maternal Connections. In: C. Ellis & A. Bochner, *Composing Ethnography: Alernative Forms of Qualitative Writing*. Lanham, MD: Altamira Press.

Ellis, C. & Bochner, A. *Composing Ethnography: Alernative Forms of Qualitative Writing*. Lanham, MD: Altamira Press.

Esterling, B.A., L'Abate, L., Murray, E.J. & Pennebaker, J.W. (1999). Empirical Foundations for Writing in Prevention and Psychotherapy: Mental and Physical Health Outcomes. *Clinical Psychology Review, 19*: 79–96.

Forster, E.M. (1927). *Aspects of the Novel*. London: Penguin, 2005.

Fox, K.V. (1996). Silent Voices: A Subversive Reading of Child Sexual Abuse. In: C. Ellis & A. Bochner, *Composing Ethnography: Alernative Forms of Qualitative Writing*. Lanham, MD: Altamira Press.

Frost, R. (1964). Letter to Louis Untermeyer. In: *Selected Letters of Robert Frost*. New York: Holt.

Gibbons, S. (1932). *Cold Comfort Farm*. London: Penguin, 1994.

Glover, J. (2005). Commentary: Socrates, Freud and Family Therapy. *Journal of Family Therapy, 27*: 392–398.

Gold, J. (2001). *Read for your Life: Literature as a Life Support System* Markham, Ontario: Fitzhenry & Whiteside.

Greenhalgh, T. & Hurwitz, B. (1998). *Narrative Based Medicine: Dialogue and Discourse in Clinical Practice*. London: British Medical Journal.

Groden, M. Kreiswirth, M. & Szeman, I. (2005). *The Johns Hopkins Guide to Literary Theory and Criticism*. Baltimore: Johns Hopkins University Press.

Hartill, G. (1998). The Web of Words: Collaborative Writing and Mental Health. In: C. Hunt & F. Sampson (Eds.), *The Self on the Page: Theory and Practice of Creative Writing in Personal Development*. London: Jessica Kingsley.

Heaney, S. (1966). Digging. In: *Death of a Naturalist*. London: Faber & Faber, 2006.

Hoffman, L. (1993). Constructing Realities: an Art of Lenses. In: *Exchanging Voices: a Collaborative Approach to Family Therapy*. London: Karnac.

Hunt, C. (2000). *Therapeutic Dimensions of Autobiography in Creative Writing*. London: Jessica Kingsley.

Hunt, C. (2004). Reading Ourselves: Imagining the Reader in the Writing Process. In: G. Bolton, S. Howlett, C. Lago & J.K. Wright (Eds.), *Writing Cures: an Introductory Handbook of Writing in Counselling and Therapy* Hove: Brunner-Routledge.

Hunt, C. & Sampson, F. (1998). *The Self on the Page: Theory and Practice of Creative Writing in Personal Development*. London: Jessica Kingsley.

Hunt, C. & Sampson, F. (2005). *Writing: Self and Reflexivity*. Basingstoke: Palgrave Macmillan.

Iser, W. (1974). The Reading Process. In: R. Cohen (Ed.), *New Directions in Literary History*. Baltimore: Johns Hopkins University Press.

Iser, W. (1978). *The Act of Reading: A Theory of Aesthetic Response*. Baltimore: Johns Hopkins University Press.

Iser, W. (1989). *Prospecting: from Reader Response to Literary Anthropology*. Baltimore: Johns Hopkins University Press.

Jamison, K.R. (1996). *Touched with Fire: Manic-Depressive Illness and the Artistic Temperament*. New York: Simon & Shuster.

Jamison, K.R. (1997). *An Unquiet Mind: a Memoir of Moods and Madness*. New York: Picador.

Janesick, Valerie, J. (1998). *"Stretching" Exercises for Qualitative Researchers*. Thousand Oaks, CA: Sage.

Jennings, S. (1998). *Introduction to Dramatherapy*. London: Jessica Kingsley.

Jung, C.G. (1989). *Memories, Dreams, Reflections*. London: Fontana.

Keats, J. (1817). Letter to George and Thomas Keats. In: H.E. Rollins (Ed.), *Letters of John Keats (1958) Vol 1*. Boston: Harvard University Press.

Keeney, B.P. (1983). *Aesthetics of Change*. New York: Guilford.

King, S. (1982). The Body. In: *Different Seasons*. London: Hodder, 2007.

King, S. (2006). *Lisey's Story*. London: Hodder.

Lacan, J. (1949). The Mirror Stage as Formative of the Function of the I as Revealed in Psychoanalytic Experience. In: V.B. Leitch (Ed.), *The Norton Anthology of Theory and Criticism* (pp. 1285–1290). London: Norton.

Lakoff, G. & Johnson, M. (1980). *Metaphors We Live By*. Chicago: University of Chicago Press.

Lakoff, G. & Turner, M. (1989). *More than Cool Reason: A Field Guide to Poetic Metaphor*. Chicago: University of Chicago Press.

Lee, H. (1960). *To Kill a Mockingbird*. London: Arrow Books, 1997.

Lee, H. (2000). Introduction. In: V. Woolf, *To the Lighthouse*. London: Penguin.

Lieblich, A., Tuval-Mashiach, R. & Zilber, T. (1998). Narrative Research: Reading, Analysis and Interpretation. *Applied Social Research Methods Series Volume 47*. Thousand Oaks, CA: Sage.

Linstone, H. & Turoff, M. (1975). *The Delphi Method: Techniques and Applications*. Reading, MA: Addison Wesley.

Lowe, G. (2000). Reading and Writing: Pleasure, Guilt and Health. *Context 47*. Association for Family Therapy.

Lowe, G. (2004). Cognitive Psychology and the Biomedical Foundations of Writing Therapy. In: G. Bolton, S. Howlett, C. Lago & J.K. Wright (Eds.), *Writing Cures: an Introductory Handbook of Writing in Counselling and Therapy*. Hove: Brunner-Routledge.

Malouf, D. (1984). *Harland's Half Acre*. London: Chatto & Windus.

Maturana, H. & Varela, F.J. (1980). *Autopoiesis and Cognition: the Realization of the Living*. Dordrecht: D. Reidel.

McLeod, J. (1997). *Narrative and Psychotherapy*. London: Sage.

Miall, D.S. & Kuiken, D. (1995). Aspects of Literary Response: A New Questionnaire. *Research in the Teaching of English, 29*: 37–58.

Miall, D.S. & Kuiken, D. (2002). A Feeling for Fiction: Becoming What we Behold. *Poetics, 30*: 221–241.

Morrison, T. (1993). Nobel Lecture. www.nobelprize.org

O'Reilly, M. (2005). The Complaining Client and the Troubled Therapist: a Discursive Investigation of Family Therapy. *Journal of Family Therapy, 27*: 370–392.

Palazzoli, M.S., Boscolo, L., Cecchin, G. & Prata, G. (1980). Hypothesizing—Circularity—Neutrality: Three Guidelines for the Conductor of the Session. *Family Process, 19*: 3–12.

Penn, P. (2004). Aesthetic Knowledge. *Context, 75*: 31–36.

Penn, P. & Frankfurt, M. (1994). Creating a Participant Text: Writing, Multiple Voices, Narrative Multiplicity. *Family Process, 33*: 217–231.

Pennebaker, J.W. (1997). Writing about Emotional Experiences as Therapeutic Process. *Psychological Science, 18*: 167–169.

Pennebaker, J.W., Kiecolt-Glaser, J.K. & Glaser, R. (1988). Disclosure of Traumas and Immune Functions: Health Implications for

Psychotherapy. *Journal of Consulting and Clinical Psychology,* 56: 239–245.

Petit, P. (2001). *The Zoo Father.* Bridgend: Poetry Wales Press.

Philipp, R. (1996). The Links between Poetry and Healing. *The Therapist, 3:* 4–15.

Philipp, R. (1997). Evaluating the Effectiveness of the Arts in Health Care. In: C. Kaye & T. Blee (Eds.), *The Arts in Health Care: A Palette of Possibilities* (pp. 250–261). London: Jessica Kingsley.

Philipp, R. (1999). Evaluating the Arts in Health Care and Mental Health Promotion—the example of creative writing. In: D. Haldane & S. Loppert (Eds.), *The Arts in Health Care: Learning from Experience* (pp. 96–114). London: King's Fund.

Philipp, R., Coppell, K. & Freeman, H. (1996). Poetry and the Art of Medicine. *British Medical Journal, 308:* 63.

Pound, E. (1913). A Few Don'ts by an Imagiste. *Poetry Magazine,* 198–206.

Pound, E. (1977). In a Station of the Metro. In: *Selected Poems 1908–1969.* London: Faber & Faber.

Richardson, L. (2000). Writing: A Method of Inquiry. In: N.K. Denzin & Y.S. Lincoln (Eds.), *Handbook of Qualitative Research.* Thousand Oaks, CA: Sage.

Rober, P. (1999). The Therapist's Inner Conversation in Family Therapy Practice: Some Ideas About the Self of the Therapist, Therapeutic Impasse, and the Process of Reflection. *Family Process, 38:* 209–227.

Romanyshyn, R.D. (2001). *Mirror and Metaphor: Images and Stories of Psychological Life.* Pittsburgh: Trivium.

Rosenblatt, P.C. (1994). *Metaphors of Family Systems Therapy: Toward New Constructions.* New York: Guilford.

Ryle, A. (2004). Writing by Patients and Therapists in Cognitive Analytic Therapy. In: G. Bolton, S. Howlett, C. Lago & J.K. Wright (Eds.), *Writing Cures: an Introductory Handbook of Writing in Counselling and Therapy.* Hove: Brunner-Routledge.

Sampson, F. (1997). Some Questions of Identity: What is Writing in Health Care? In: C. Kaye & T. Blee (Eds.), *The Arts in Health Care: A Palette of Possibilities.* London: Jessica Kingsley.

Shotter, J. & Gergen, K.J. (1993). *Texts of Identity.* London: Sage.

Smith, K. & Sweeney, M. (1997). *Beyond Bedlam: Poems Written out of Mental Distress.* London: Anvil Press.

Smyth, J.M., Stone, A.A., Hurewitz, A. & Kaell, A. (1999). Effects of Writing about Stressful Experiences on Symptom Reduction in Patients with Asthma or Rheumatoid Arthritis: A Randomized Trial. *Journal of the American Medical Association, 281:* 1304–1309.

Snyder, M. (1996). Our "Other History": Poetry as a Meta-Metaphor for Narrative Therapy. *Journal of Family Therapy*, 337–361.

Tillmann-Healey, L.M. (1996). A Secret Life in a Culture of Thinness: Reflections on Body, Food and Bulimia. In: C. Ellis & A. Bochner, *Composing Ethnography: Alernative Forms of Qualitative Writing*. Lanham, MD: Altamira Press.

Tomm, K. (1987). Interventive Interviewing: Parts I and II. *Family Process*, 26: 3–13, 167–83.

Tomm, K. (1988). Interventive Interviewing: Part III. Intending to Ask Lineal, Circular, Strategic or Reflexive Questions. *Family Process*, 27: 1–15.

Turner, M. (1996). *The Literary Mind: the Origins of Thought and Language*. New York: Oxford University Press.

Vetere, A. & Dowling, E. (2005). *Narrative Therapies with Children and their Families*. Hove: Routledge.

Watzlawick, P., Beavin-Bavelas, J. & Jackson, D. (1967). A Communicational Approach to the Play *Who's Afraid of Virginia Woolf?* In: *Pragmatics of Human Communication: a Study of Interactional Patterns, Pathologies and Paradoxes*. New York: Norton.

White, M. (1992). Family Therapy Training and Supervision in a World of Experience and Narrative. In: D. Epston & M. White (Eds.), *Experience, Contradiction, Narrative and Imagination*. Adelaide: Dulwich Center Publications.

White, M. (2007). *Maps of Narrative Practice*. New York: Norton.

White, M. & Epston, D. (1990). *Narrative Means to Therapeutic Ends*. New York: Norton.

Woolf, V. (1927). Letter to Roger Fry, May 27th.

Woolf, V. (1985). *Moments of Being: a Collection of Autobiographical Writing*. Orlando, FA: Harcourt.

Woolf, V. (1927). *To the Lighthouse*. London: Penguin Classics, 1992.

Wright, J.K. (2004). The Passion of Science, the Precision of Poetry: Therapeutic Writing—a Review of the Literature. In: G. Bolton, S. Howlett, C. Lago & J.K. Wright (Eds.), *Writing Cures: an Introductory Handbook of Writing in Counselling and Therapy*. Hove: Brunner-Routledge.

Zunshine, L. (2006). *Why we Read Fiction: Theory of Mind and the Novel*. Columbus: Ohio State University Press.

List of literary works mentioned in the text and not included in the references

Books

Aeschylus: *Oresteia*
Albee, Edward: *Who's afraid of Virginia Woolf?*
Anancy stories: books, cassettes and CDs all available on the internet
Angelou, Maya: *I Know Why the Caged Bird Sings*
Atwood, Margaret: *The Handmaid's Tale*
Austen, Jane: *Pride and Prejudice*
Ba, Mariama: *Une Si Longue Lettre*
Breeze, Jean "Binta": *The Arrival of Brighteye*
Bronte, Charlotte: *Jane Eyre*
Bronte, Emily: *Wuthering Heights*
Collins, Wilkie: *The Moonstone*
Collins, Wilkie: *The Woman in White*
Conrad, Joseph: *Heart of Darkness*
Davies, W.H.: *Leisure*
Deane, Seamus: *Reading in the Dark*
Defoe, Daniel: *Journal of the Plague Year*
Du Maurier, Daphne: *Rebecca*
Eliot, George: *The Mill on the Floss*

Fielding, Helen: *Bridget Jones's Diary*
Faulkner, William: *The Sound and the Fury*
Fitzgerald, F. Scott: *The Great Gatsby*
Forster, E.M.: *Howards End*
Gibran, Kahlil: *The Prophet*
Grossmith, George and Weedon: *Diary of a Nobody*
Haddon, Mark: *The Curious Incident of the Dog in the Night Time*
Heaney, Seamus: *Beowulf* (translation)
Homer: *Iliad*
Homer: *Odyssey*
Hughes, Ted: *Birthday letters*
Jhabvala, Ruth Prawer: *Heat and Dust*
James, Henry: *Washington Square*
Joyce, James: *Ulysses*
Kafka, Franz: *Metamorphosis*
King, Stephen: *Dreamcatcher*
King, Stephen: *The Dark Half*
Kureishi, Hanif: *The Buddha of Suburbia*
Laclos, P.C.: *Les Liaisons Dangereuses*
Levi, Primo: *If This is a Man*
Mason, Mala: *Survivor*
Matheson, Richard: *I am Legend*
McEwan, Ian: *Enduring Love*
McEwan, Ian: *Saturday*
Michaels, Anne: *Fugitive Pieces*
Miller, Arthur: *All My Sons*
Mitchell, Margaret: *Gone with the Wind*
Nabokov, Vladimir: *Lolita*
Nafisi, Azar: *Reading* Lolita *in Tehran*
Owen, Wilfred: *The Parable of the Old Man and the Young*
Pepys, Samuel: *Diary*
Petit, Pascale: *A Parcel of Land*
Petit, Pascale: *Frozen Falls*
Petit, Pascale: *Eisriesenfeld*
Pope, Alexander: *Essay on Criticism*
Potter, Beatrix: *The Tale of Two Bad Mice*
Proulx, Annie: *The Shipping News*
Read, Piers Paul: *Alive: the Story of the Andes Survivors*

Richardson, Samuel: *Clarissa*
Richardson, Samuel: *Pamela*
Rushdie, Salman: *Midnight's Children*
Sanskrit poems: *Ramayana* and *Mahabharata*
Salinger, J.D.: *The Catcher in the Rye*
Sassoon, Siegfried: *Memoirs of a Foxhunting Man*
Sebold, Alice: *The Lovely Bones*
Shakespeare, William: *Romeo and Juliet*
Shakespeare, William: *King Lear*
Shakespeare, William: *Hamlet*
Shriver, Lionel: *We Need to Talk About Kevin*
Simpson, Joe: *Touching the Void*
Sophocles: *Antigone*
Spufford, Francis: *The Child that Books Built*
Steinbeck, John: *The Grapes of Wrath*
Stevenson, Robert Louis: *The Strange Case of Dr. Jekyll and Mr. Hyde*
Stevenson, Robert Louis: *Treasure Island*
Stoker, Bram: *Dracula*
Sumerian text: *Epic of Gilgamesh*
Tennyson, Alfred: *The Lady of Shalott*
Townsend, Sue: *Adrian Mole* novels
Urquhart, Jane: *The Whirlpool*
Varley, Susan: *Badger's Parting Gifts*
Walker, Alice: *The Color Purple*
White, E.B.: *Charlotte's Web*
Wordsworth, William: *The Prelude*
Wordsworth, William: *Upon Westminster Bridge*

Films and TV

Bill and Ted's Bogus Journey
Dallas
Dreamcatcher
EastEnders
The Exorcist
Final Destination (1–3)
The Incredible Hulk—film and TV versions
The Simpsons (almost any episode)
X Files

Songs

Gaynor, Gloria: *I Will Survive*
Lloyd, Marie: *A Little of What you Fancy Does you Good*

Paintings

De Chirico: *The Uncertainty of the Poet*

Literary texts brought by research participants

This is a list, for your interest and information, of literature/writers mentioned by respondents to Questionnaire 1, which was part of the Delphi in the study *An Exploration of the Place of Literary Reading in Family Therapists' Personal and Professional Development* (Burns, 2003). It is arranged roughly according to the order of the sections of Questionnaire 1 but is not otherwise in any particular order. Some texts are named by several people and occur in different sections, but no attempt has been made to indicate frequencies and/or the degree of significance attached by respondents to the literature mentioned.

Childhood

Fairy tales
Stories made up by parent(s)
Stories told by grandparent(s)—about own life
Poetry recited by grandparent(s)
Enid Blyton: *Noddy; Famous Five; Secret Seven; Hurrah for the Circus*
A.A. Milne: *Winnie the Pooh; When we were Very Young; Now we are Six*
Going Shopping: first book about children from different countries
Hungarian folk tales

American folk tales
Toytown (radio)
Children's Hour (radio)
Own stories
Biblical stories
Greek, Roman and Norse myths
Pony books
Encyclopaedias
Arthur Mee's Children's Encyclopaedia
Kipling
Nevil Shute
Jules Verne
Agatha Christie
Sci-Fi
Comics: *Dandy, Topper, Lion, Rover, Beano*
R.L. Stevenson: *Treasure Island*
Anthony Buckeridge: *Jennings* books
Frank Richards: *Billy Bunter* books
Jerome K. Jerome: *Three Men in a Boat*
Conan Doyle
L.M. Montgomery: *Anne of Green Gables*
Carolyn Keene: *Nancy Drew* books
Noel Streatfield: *A Vicarage Family; The New Town*
Louisa May Alcott: *Little Women*
Kate Seredy: *The Good Master*
Susan Coolidge: *What Katy Did*
Anna Sewell: *Black Beauty*
Capt. W.E. Johns: *Biggles* books
Biography, e.g. Marie Curie

Adolescence

Tolkien: *Lord of the Rings; The Hobbit*
C.S. Lewis (*Narnia? Screwtape Letters?*)
Georgette Heyer: romantic novels and light historical fiction
Science fiction
Ian Fleming: *James Bond* novels
Cynthia Harnett: *The Wool-Pack*

Louisa May Alcott: *Little Women*
D.H. Lawrence: *Sons and Lovers*
Jules Verne
Conan Doyle
George Orwell, including *Animal Farm*
Victor Hugo
Mark Twain
Daniel Defoe
Arthur C. Clarke
P.G. Wodehouse
Shakespeare
Dickens
Fielding
Herman Melville: *Moby Dick*
War stories (non-fiction)
Satirical tales
Poetry: Dylan Thomas, Wordsworth, Eliot, Chaucer
Books on motor racing and cars
Plays and drama
Biggles books
Love stories
Adventures ("doctor hero stuff")
Thrillers
A.J. Cronin
George Eliot
E.F. Benson
Hemingway
Anna Sewell: *Black Beauty*
J.D. Salinger: *The Catcher in the Rye*
Classic novels
"Anything forbidden"
Mary O'Hara: *My Friend Flicka; Thunderhead; Green Grass of Wyoming*
Series of family sagas, e.g. Mazo de la Roche: *Jalna*
Jane Austen: *Pride and Prejudice*
Emily Bronte: *Wuthering Heights*
Charlotte Bronte: *Jane Eyre*
Agatha Christie
James Baldwin: *Another Country; Giovanni's Room*

Young adulthood

Marilynn French novels, e.g. *The Women's Room*
Germaine Greer
Betty Friedan
William Golding: *Lord of the Flies*
Vincent (biographical novel of Vincent Van Gogh)
Axel Munthe: *Story of San Michele*
Autobiography, e.g. Bertrand Russell
Erich Fromm: *Art of Loving*
R.D. Laing: *Divided Self*
Jung: *Integrity of the Personality*
W. Somerset Maugham: *Of Human Bondage*
Chaucer; Herman Hesse; Huxley; Timothy Leary
Bateson
Kerouac
Ken Kesey: *One Flew over the Cuckoo's Nest*
Tom Wolfe: *Electric Kool Aid Acid Test*
Metaphysical poets: John Donne, George Herbert
Agatha Christie
French Existentialism: Sartre, Simone de Beauvoir
Margaret Attwood; Iris Murdoch; Angela Carter; Doris Lessing; John
    Fowles
Patrick White; Colin Wilson; Alvin Toffler; Arthur Koestler; Albert
    Camus
Black American political writing: Cleaver, Baldwin
Graham Greene
John Le Carré
James Joyce
Françoise Sagan
Tolstoy; Dostoevsky
Gerard Manley Hopkins: poetry

Current reading

Work (academic psychology, systems/family theory, family therapy
    research)
John Steinbeck
Irvine Welsh: *Trainspotting*; Sharpe novels

Chaucer; Hardy; Hugo; Dostoevsky; Solzhenitsyn; Galsworthy
Biography/autobiography
Crime writers, e.g. P.D. James
Margaret Atwood; Peter Hoeg; Armistead Maupin; David Lodge
Joanna Trollope
Thomas Hardy
Jeannette Winterson; Alice Walker
Intelligent thriller, e.g. Peter Akroyd: *Dan Leno and the Limehouse Golem*
Michael Dibdin: *Cosi fan Tutti*
Roddy Doyle: *The Woman Who Walked Into Doors*
George Eliot: *Daniel Deronda*
A.L. Kennedy: *Original Bliss*
Bernard Malamud: *Dubin's Lives*
May Sarton: *House by the Sea* (autobiography)
History, especially World Wars 1 and 2
Biography/autobiography, e.g. Brian Keenan: *An Evil Cradling*
Eric Lomax: *The Railway Men*
Bert Keizer: *Dancing with Mr. D*
Philippa Pearce: *Tom's Midnight Garden*
Sebastian Faulks: *Birdsong*
Newspapers, *Private Eye*
Louis de Bernières: *Captain Corelli's Mandolin*
Doris Lessing (autobiography)
Jane Smiley; Helen Dunmore; Carol Shields; Ann Tyler; Eva Hoffman
"Classics": George Eliot, Henry James, Wilkie Collins
Black women's writing: Maya Angelou, Toni Morrison, Alice Walker
Poems: Carol Ann Duffy, Liz Lochhead
Stendhal
Arundhati Roy: *God of Small Things*

Reading together with children

Made-up stories
C.S. Lewis
Roald Dahl
Poetry (Liverpool poets); Brian Patten's children's poetry
Tolkien; Conan Doyle; Grimm's Fairy Tales; Arabian Nights; Shakespeare
Wizard of Oz

P.L. Travers: *Mary Poppins*
George Orwell: *Animal Farm*
Oscar Wilde: *The Happy Prince*
Stig of the Dump
Jonathan Swift: *Gulliver's Travels*
Black Beauty
Greek, Celtic, Nordic myths
Alice in Wonderland

Significant and/or useful book/film

R. Dinnage: *The Ruffian on the Stair* (bereavement)
C.S. Lewis: *A Grief Observed* (bereavement)
Judith Guest: *Ordinary People*
Babette's Feast (film)
Ibsen: *Pillars of the Community*
Ustinov: *Photo Finish*
Sartre: *Kean*
Citizen Kane (film)
Steinbeck: *Grapes of Wrath*
Peter Hoeg: *Borderlines*
Keri Hume: *The Bone People*
Janet Frame: *An Angel at my Table*
Padre Padrone (film)
Poetry of Gerard Manley Hopkins
George Eliot: *The Mill on the Floss*
Poems of Louis MacNeice
Sophocles: *Oedipus the King*
Edward Albee: *Who's Afraid of Virginia Woolf?*

APPENDIX 3

Literary resources and how to find them

In the Introduction I explained the benefits of having your own literary text beside you. It is increasingly easy to access the majority of material, including most of the texts referred to in this book, although occasionally you may have to work a little harder to find a specific example, especially if it is out of print.

Online

This advice is greatly simplified, thanks to the internet. For poems, it is often enough to enter the first line into your search engine and wait. Novels may be more difficult unless your extract contains a much quoted passage. Even so, try to enter a line and see what happens. Since it is often a quotation which comes to mind first, this strategy can be helpful in signposting you to the right place, even if the whole text is not provided. You may want to try the following:

* The Poetry Library (www.poetrylibrary.co.uk), South Bank Centre, London. The Poetry Library has a wide range of services, resources, and events. It also provides an online Newsletter.

- Voice of the Shuttle (http://vos.ucsb.edu) is a huge, well established website which supplies links to electronic texts and other resources for English and American Literature.
- Project Gutenberg (www.gutenberg.com) offers 17000 e-books (copyright expired in USA) to download. These include Joyce's *Ulysses*, the *Iliad* and *Odyssey*, Slave Narratives, *Beowulf*, and many more texts mentioned in this book.
- http://poetry.about.com offers help in reading and accessing poetry texts.

Libraries

If you prefer more personal guidance and an actual book to hold, your local library may be the place of choice. The librarian is trained to help with locating what you want and indicating new routes of exploration. There is no substitute for having the book in your hands: its appearance and feel are important parts of the experience. Browsing poetry books or anthologies can often lead you to other items you might enjoy and find helpful, and the same is true of a novel, although reading the whole thing is obviously the ideal. Reading twice (or more) can also be a revelation, especially if the last time you read, say, Daphne du Maurier's *Rebecca* was when you were 14. Librarians are likely to be sympathetic with the project outlined in this book. Bibliotherapy services are often based in libraries, although in the UK these may offer predominantly self-help literature, rather than "literary" works.

Reference texts like the *Oxford Companion to English Literature*, *Oxford Companion to Children's Literature* and *Chambers Dictionary of Literary Characters* can be a great help in finding a way through the huge variety of literature on offer. Don't forget, also, anthologies of poetry and prose and the many "Readers" which give selections of useful texts for students from medieval to contemporary literature written in English. Translations are also widely available of literature from other languages both ancient and modern, as are "post-colonial" texts which arise out of, and allow engagement with, productions from a variety of contemporary cultures.

Buying texts

Being able to keep texts for future reference in their original bindings might be considered a luxury, but I would recommend it highly. Not only is it a way of getting some reward to the writers but it opens the way to browsing your own bookshelves. This activity, as noted in Chapter Seven, amounts to a technique for personal development. New texts supply their own frisson of excitement, but the increasing array of second-hand book buying on the internet makes it possible to locate specific texts at attractive prices.

Radio and TV

Literature is discussed on both radio and TV, and it is often possible to locate a particular text using websites and "listen again" facilities.

Exercises

The exercises set out below are designed to promote more creative, responsive and versatile ways of thinking and feeling rather than to provide answers to pressing questions. They are all given a rough structure, but are intended to be modified to suit different conditions, and whilst there are many advantages to working with others, most can be adapted for use alone. Time is often a constraint, and although most of the exercises benefit from up to an hour of dedicated time, this too can be flexible. Where specific texts are suggested, it may only be possible to provide an extract. There are huge benefits for those who are prepared to take a little time and effort to find the relevant texts in full (see *A note about literary texts*).

Introductory exercise: a "reading history"

This exercise is an exploration of the notion that because we can form deep attachments to literary texts, surveying the pattern of our attachments over time can provide significant insights into our personal development. This exercise asks participants to consider their developmental history in relation to their current experience of training as a family therapist. It acts as a "warm up" for all the other exercises in the book, but please bear in mind that thinking about your reading experiences from the past can carry a surprising emotional charge. Make sure to look after yourself and look out for others who may be doing the exercise with you.

Working with a partner, begin to think together about the stories, books, poems, songs, plays etc. which you remember from the past and which have been significant for you. So as not to get "stuck" in one period of life, try to go through chronologically, remembering to take turns and note down anything which particularly strikes you as you go. Since you are working in twos you can help each other by pointing out any significance which strikes you about your partner's account—they may not be able to notice it themselves!

- Begin with childhood/pre-school if you can—the first thing you remember reading or being read (or told) to you. What was special about it then? What continuing significance can you detect now?
- Later childhood and adolescence—the period of reading alongside school friends perhaps, or beginning to get a taste for a particular type of fiction or character. Maybe also the period of giving up on story books and moving on to something else. What was important to you then? What significance has this now?
- Adulthood—how have your reading preferences developed? If not reading then what else? Film? TV? Work only? What are your reflections on this for yourself and your partner?
- Current reading—what has interested you recently (might be a whole novel or just a few words)? How does this link with your current training experiences?
- How does the developmental history you have constructed link with the personal professional development you are working on now, in this course?
- Sum up with your partner and then, if there is the opportunity, share with the bigger group.

Exercise 1: Head and heart

This exercise is designed to help participants develop their abilities in multi-level (intellectual; emotional; philosophical; embodied/practical) engagement.

Working in pairs, one person begins by relating a challenging experience. This should be something which has left you at a bit of a loss to know what to do and how to feel. Be careful to use only what you are prepared to share. Next you will need to identify a short poem. This one by Adrienne Rich has been included here because it has proved particularly evocative for a number of groups:

Delta

If you have taken this rubble for my past
raking through it for fragments you could sell
know that I long ago moved on
deeper into the heart of the matter

If you think you can grasp me, think again:
my story flows in more than one direction
a delta springing from the riverbed
with its five fingers spread

- Begin with a careful reading of your poem. It is often good to read poems aloud, whether you are working on your own or with others. Consider the title and what it suggests to you. You may be a person who works best by visualising so allow yourself to create some images either in your mind's eye, or by actually drawing, if that is better. Look at what is being said in succeeding lines/verses.
- Next, turn to your neighbour (if you have one) and exchange your thoughts about what you think the poet is getting at.
- Then exchange ideas of what this poem says to you personally. If this does not come easily, you might help each other with prompts such as: have you ever felt imprisoned or limited by other people's ideas about you? How would you want people to see you, recognise your worth, respect your integrity? Personally? Professionally?
- Consider what emotions are attached to this. Allow yourself to wander amongst different responses as you listen and talk. What does the poet suggest as a solution? How does this fit for you in your current personal/professional life? What do you think about it? What do you feel about it? What might you do about it?
- Finally, return to your original dilemma or challenging experience. Note any differences in how you position yourself after the discussion you have had, and listen to the comments of your discussion partner.

Exercise 2: Enriching therapeutic discourse

This exercise builds on the idea that reflecting on a literary example, with a personal or work issue in mind, can extend the range of ideas, solutions, inspirations which may apply. The point is not to provide ready-made answers but to increase your range of options and your reflexive awareness. It is, therefore, an invitation to bring more creativity into both theoretical and practical discourses.

• Working on your own if you have to or with one or two others if you can, think of a therapeutic intervention which you use, or have seen used, to good effect.
• Next, think of a therapeutic intervention or technique of which you are suspicious.
• Next, without trying too hard, or trying for too exact a match, see if there is a story, character, poem, quotation, proverb, image, etc. which comes to mind in connection with either or both. What emotions does the image or story bring forth in you? What draws you to it or what do you find worthy of dislike or suspicion? Write these down if you are working on your own.
• Next, return to the therapeutic item you identified—what is there in your thinking now which diverges most from your initial position? You might also want to revisit this question after a few days or weeks.

Exercise 3: Pick a metaphor!

Metaphors can guide our thinking in ways which may surprise us. Since metaphors often operate at a level below that of our conscious attention, they can limit as well as extend our range. This exercise represents an attempt to harness the energy and power of metaphors through the conscious exploration of literary examples.

Complete the following:

• *On a good day I see myself as a therapist who somewhat resembles/has characteristics of…* Choose a literary character (e.g. Sherlock Holmes, Harry Potter, Superman, Flora Poste from *Cold Comfort Farm*) or motif (e.g. The Raven, A Grecian Urn) or something/someone more suitable of your own choice.
• *With this likeness in mind I would like to develop my therapeutic skills in these directions …* Reply with your "role model" in mind—even if your answers seem a bit outrageous. This reflection is just for you.

- Finally take a step back and think of how the persona and the skills you mention could be used in the setting in which you work. What adjustments would be necessary to achieve a fit?

If you can do this exercise in the company of others, take some time to compare notes and make suggestions to each other. This is an opportunity to focus on a literary character or object of reflection to develop ideas in unexpected directions.

If, for example, you have chosen the poem "The Road Less Travelled" by Robert Frost, and you are contemplating "Two roads diverge in a yellow wood", try to let your reflections be led by the image this presents and then apply this to your therapeutic practice rather than the other way round—what are the roads like? What are the dangers of taking one or the other, what the advantages? Do you mind if you get lost? What sort of footwear do you have on your feet? Is it a sunny morning or the end of a wet afternoon? Let your imagination run away for ten minutes or so. Only then try to tie it back down to your practice.

Exercise 4: Literary "maps"

It is surprising how often a story, character or particular literary genre (detective fiction perhaps, or comic books) can influence our development long after we have forgotten, or apparently "grown out of" them. Revisiting these roots can sometimes help us to regain the energy of the past or, alternatively, help us to move on. This exercise is good to do with a partner or in a group, but it is also a good one to do on your own.

- Let your mind wander back into earlier phases of your life and the kind of reading or storytelling you remember. For many people this means myths and legends or fairy stories. For others there might be favourite characters and stories in books, comics, film or television.
- Identify one character/story that you remember. What do you think makes this story or character memorable for you?
- What do you see as the main motivation/driving force of your chosen character/story? What moves the story along?
- How do these motivations relate to your own? Do they relate to you more in your personal or your professional life or at one period of your development rather than another?

- Write your conclusions down and revisit from time to time to see what else this memory may have to say to you about your own development, past, present and future.

Exercise 5: Sharing the load

This exercise draws on the natural externalising qualities of literature and composed images to create a context which enables the sharing of difficult topics, i.e. it is both challenging and safe. It is based directly on the findings of the research exercise referred to in Chapter Five. It is important to try to do this exercise with others if possible, and in the absence of a facilitator, one person should be asked to volunteer to do the preparation and also keep an eye on important boundaries such as time, turn taking, etc.

Preparation

The leader or designated member of the group should already have prepared some brief quotations and/or images relating to traumatic events. It is essential for these to be "composed", i.e. a poem, a painting or a photograph which is intended to stand alone and be valuable for itself, so look in anthologies or published collections of images. It would not be helpful simply to subject group members to grisly pictures of injuries, whereas a Francis Bacon painting or some war photography could be very evocative in a creative way. A degree of composition sets the image or words in a context and provides some distance between the subject and the observer—this is a safer as well as a more productive form. The death of Anna Karenina, as another example, is extremely involving and shocking, but is clearly placed within the frame of the novel of the same name. The leader needs to provide two "hats" and put the quotations/images in one of them.

Next:

- Each person in the group should think individually for a moment about a clinical topic or personal/professional situation which they find particularly intimidating to talk about because of its emotional impact, e.g. the deaths of children, loss of independence (as in quadriplegia, dementia, etc.), feeling of personal incompetence in training, and so on. Each person is to write down their own example and place it in the empty "hat".

- Each person should now take a slip from each "hat". If you get your own, please put it back and take another.
- Everyone take a few minutes to think about the two slips and the relationship between them.
- The first person to see a connection between the difficult topic and the quotation or image should present it to the group. It isn't necessary to look for positives at this stage; in fact it is important to stay with the discomfort, disgust or pain for the time being. Each person has handed their discomfort to another, so it is important to try to enter as fully as possible into difficulty of the situation or topic.
- Each person in the group should have a roughly similar amount of time to present their reflections.
- The group then gives reflections on the reflections, and this is the time for positives, encouragement and cross-fertilisation between different experiences. Individuals should feel free to "own up" to their "discomforting situation" or not.

NB: please note that most, or all, of the discussion may centre on the quotation or image and not on the personal pain or discomfort. This is part of the "externalising" propensity of literary discussion.

Exercise 6: Several ways to get writing!

Getting started

Gillie Bolton has many wise words of guidance for people who want to begin reflective writing. I have borrowed this advice from her (Bolton, 2005):

- This writing is yours and is private until you choose to share it with another.
- Trust the authority of the writing hand.
- Thinking inhibits creativity, believe it or not. Let it flow.
- Suspend your disbelief.
- Your writing is a gift to yourself.
- You can't write the wrong thing. Whatever you write will be right—or you.
- Forget about grammar, syntax, spelling—for now. Worrying about them blocks the inspirational flow. Correct them later.
- Trust the process; have faith in yourself.

I have also borrowed these exercises from her and adapted them for our purposes. These exercises are all better done as part of a group. The first two exercises are really warm ups to get you into the writing mood and alert you to possible perspectives you have not noticed before. You may want to go on to some more focused writing afterwards, e.g. your reflective journal, a case study, a training course assignment, an article you are writing, etc. Allow yourself enough time to relax with these exercises. It may be wise to spread them out and not to try to do everything at the same time.

From another point of view

Write a five minute piece from the point of view of

- The chair you sit in when meeting with clients
- The one-way screen in your family therapy suite (if you have one)
- The car you drive to your work/training course
- Your CD player

Read back to yourself and share with others in your group. Comment briefly and appreciatively.

Milestones

- List the milestones of your life and/or career—*very quickly*.
- Read back to yourself: delete or add, clarify or expand as you wish.
- Delete all the obvious things or things other people would know; try to add instead some not very obvious things or things only you know about, e.g. the first time you really felt you put a difficult idea from your theory base into practice, the last time you read a book/poem or saw a film which changed your life.

Read carefully to yourself and share what you have written with your group—appreciatively.

Listing

This exercise can be used to lead into a longer exercise which involves composing a poem from the product of the lists and also possibly "found" items. Very quickly, and without too much thought, list 20 things which make you:

- Pleased with your progress on the course/in your professional development
- Worried about your progress on the course/in your professional development
- Glad to be training/working as a therapy practitioner

This will produce approximately 60 items—do more if you want to and have time. Don't hold back from writing down silly things/weird things/things you would like to keep to yourself—you are not going to have to feed them back. If you go on to make a poem from the raw ingredients, this will be the time to share with others.

Exercise 7: Famous last words

This exercise gives an opportunity to attend to the kinds of internal conversations which may have influenced us during a piece of work. It is a quick exercise to do when you have used up all your energy and time in doing all the other exercises in the book! It will also work fine for the ending of a piece of work. Again, do it with others if you can, or if not, on your own, using your own reflections in the shared steps.

- Each person takes a few moments to think of a fictional character they would have liked to accompany them through the task which has just finished. It may be that this character has been in the background all along or it may have to be thought about for the first time.
- Now think what parting accolade, or positive observation, you would like this character to have made about your performance in the task now finished.
- In twos, share this with a neighbour.
- Together, and giving equal time to each, review the observations. Feel free to add to them from your own mutual observations.
- What parting advice might your character offer for the future?
- Use a few minutes to reflect together on the advice, and again add to it from your own observations.
- Share and enjoy.

INDEX